THE FAMILY LIBRARY OF
CATS

THE FAMILY LIBRARY OF
CATS

Grace Pond and
Jacqueline Dineen

This edition first published 1982
by Octopus Books Limited
59 Grosvenor Street
London W1

© 1981 Octopus Books Limited

ISBN 0 7064 1459 4

Produced for Octopus by
Theorem Publishing Limited

Printed in Hong Kong

Introduction

Cats are well known for remaining slightly aloof from their human owners. But even so, in Ancient Egyptian times and before, cats deigned to live in and around human settlements, taking advantage of what we could offer them in the way of food and shelter. In the past, they earned their keep by killing vermin. Today their grace and beauty still earn them a place in homes the world over.

There is now a wonderful variety of colours and breeds to choose from, which can be bewildering if you are thinking of keeping a cat for the first time. This concise and entertaining guide gives a full account of cats and their care, from the exotic pedigree show cat to the friendly family pet.

Contents

Chapter one
The History of the Cat Family

One moment purring by the fireside, a pet cat can quickly turn into a fierce hunter, poised to attack. Our sleek, well-fed pets are really not so far removed from their relations, the big cats.

A domestic cat rubbing against its owner's legs, or purring by the fire, may seem very different from a lion or a tiger. But if you watch an angry, spitting cat with its flattened ears and bared teeth, or a cat stealthily stalking its prey and pouncing for a kill, you will easily see a similarity between the domestic animal and its wild ancestors.

The cat family evolved from a small weasel-like animal called *Miacis*. It was about 50 million years before primitive man began to take an interest in the smaller varieties of cat. In time he began to catch and tame animals which could be useful to him. He realized that some animals could help him, so he did not kill them for food. The smaller members of the cat family have always eaten rodents and rodents have always been a nuisance to man. Perhaps he recognized this fact far earlier than records show. He may not have tamed cats – indeed, some breeds are untameable to this day. But perhaps he allowed wild cats to hover round his camps, scavenging for scraps of food and killing the rats and mice that raided food supplies.

Cats were obviously not particularly important to human beings at that time. They are not shown in any of the early cave pictures. This suggests that, though people may have found cats useful to have around, they had not yet become part of everyday life. How the cat became accepted into the human household must remain guesswork, because no evidence has ever been found.

One legend has it that cats were created so that Noah could have a pair of them in the Ark. What was meant by a 'cat' in these early Bible writings is not known and there is only one mention of cats in the Bible. It does not seem as if

Of all the big cats, the lion is perhaps the most majestic and powerful. Lions live in Africa and India and hunt grazing animals such as antelope and zebra. The males have fine golden manes.

the cat as a pet or rodent catcher was known to people in Old Testament times.

The cat in ancient history

The first records of domesticated cats are in Ancient Egyptian wall paintings of 5000 years ago. We can see from these paintings that the cat was an established part of daily life. Cats protected food stores and granaries from the invasion of rats and mice. They were kept as household pets, and were also used to hunt wildfowl for the table. Egyptian families often kept a hunting cat, as well as cats to kill rodents and snakes.

The types of cats common in Egyptian times have been identified from wall paintings and from mummified remains. The Jungle Cat, which lives in Africa and Asia today, was probably used for hunting. It has tabby markings on a sandy or reddish background. The Jungle Cat hunts birds, hares and some reptiles. The other type of cat which might have been tamed then is the African Wild Cat. It also has tabby markings, and is slightly bigger than the domestic cat of today.

The Egyptian Mau is a modern breed that has been carefully developed to look like the cats shown in early Egyptian wall paintings. These cats always had tabby or spotted markings, on a reddish or brown background. The cat was so highly regarded in Egypt that it became a sacred animal. Household cats wore gold jewellery encrusted with precious stones, and when one died, all the family mourned for it. The body of the dead cat would be embalmed and buried with great ceremony. In fact, a cat cemetery containing the mummified bodies of thousands of cats, has been discovered in Egypt. From this, archaeologists have learned a great deal about the species of the time.

There was even a cat goddess, and temples were built in honour of cats, whose bodies were embalmed in solid gold coffins.

Nowhere else was the cat treated with

Cats have been depicted in art for centuries, and this is one way of telling what they were like in the past. The cat in this 18th century painting looks much like a cat of today.

such honour at this time, though there is evidence that semi-domesticated cats existed in China and India during this period. Merchants and travellers visiting Egypt began to smuggle some of the tame cats back to their own countries, though this was strictly forbidden by the Egyptians. Gradually, domestic cats began to appear in other parts of the world.

It was not until the Romans began to build up their Empire that the distribution of domestic cats became widespread. The Roman armies took tame cats back to Rome with them and they were quickly put to good use as vermin controllers. The Romans began to think of cats as a vital part of their armies and took them everywhere they went. So cats were introduced all over Europe, and into Britain.

The cat as a hunter

In 936 AD, Howell the Good, king of Wales, issued a set of laws to protect cats. He set a legal price on cats. A kitten was worth one penny until its eyes opened. From then until it caught its first mouse it was worth twopence. A fully-fledged hunter was worth fourpence. For this price, a cat had to have perfect sight and hearing, and good claws. A female cat had to be able to bring up kittens and, of course, it had to be a conscientious hunter. If a purchaser found that his cat fell short of any of these qualifications, he could demand the return of one-third of the purchase price from the seller. So cats were officially recognized, and there were penalties for ill-treating, killing or stealing them.

Cats in myth and magic

Cats have always been associated with myth and magic, and because of this

The Romans brought cats over from Egypt and used them for hunting and killing vermin. This mosaic, which dates from about 100 B.C. shows a tabby type of cat catching a bird. A picture like this shows how important cats were to the Romans. They took their cats everywhere they went.

superstition their fortunes have fluctuated in Europe. On the one hand, cats have always had their practical uses. As towns and cities became more crowded, so the rat population increased, bringing disease with it. Cats were useful to keep vermin in check. The holds of ships, packed with cargo and food for a voyage, were usually infested with rats. Most ships took cats along on voyages to keep the rats under control. This also helped to distribute cats around the world as cats and kittens sometimes escaped from ships in some faraway port and stayed there.

But as well as being useful, cats were associated with strange and magical powers. It was thought that they could cure various ailments. The Celts believed that cats' eyes were windows through which the fairies were watching their every move.

It was during the Middle Ages in Europe that cats became associated with witchcraft. The black cat is always shown as the witch's companion in old and

The family tree of the cat

The family tree shows that several groups of mammal, including the cat family, share a common ancestor. This small carnivorous creature, *Miacis*, first appeared about 50 million years ago. It was a short-legged, weasel-like creature with a long body, and it ate

other, smaller animals. As the climate and vegetation on earth changed, different types of animal evolved, including more small animals which were the prey of *Miacis* and the other carnivores.

A descendant of *Miacis*, several million years later, was the sabre-

toothed tiger, *Smilodon*. It was about the size of a big cat such as a lion, with two 6-inch (15 cm) long canine teeth. It could kill the large, slow, plant-eating creatures of the time, but was too clumsy to catch the smaller, swifter creatures that were beginning to appear.

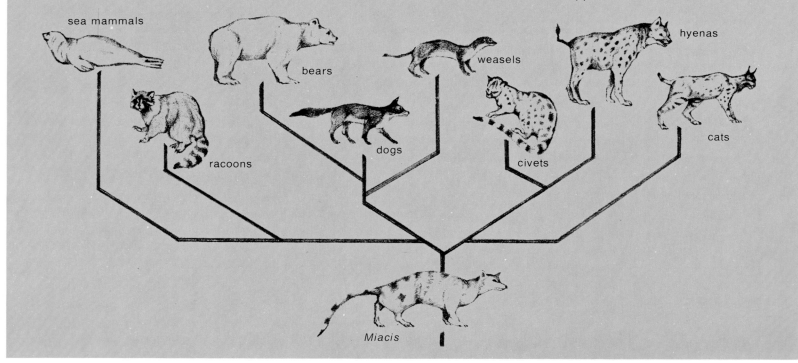

sea mammals

bears

weasels

hyenas

racoons

dogs

civets

cats

Miacis

The cheetah is one of the fastest animals alive, and so is built for speed. It is tall and slim with long legs. The cubs have fluffy coats which later turn into sleek golden with black spots. The mother cheetah has to spend most of her time hunting to feed the cubs, which need a great deal of food.

modern-day pictures. Why this started is not really known. It may simply be that women who were suspected of being witches usually lived alone and kept a cat for company. But whatever the reason, people came to believe that the cat was the Devil. Many cats were burned at the stake with the so-called witches, and others were burned or sacrificed in ritual killings.

It is said that at the coronation of Elizabeth I of England, the crowd was entertained by the burning of a wicker effigy of the Pope filled with live cats. To the people, it is said, the crying cats were 'the language of the devils within the body of the Holy Father'.

There are other horrific tales of cruelty, such as the roasting of a live cat to turn bad luck into good.

People hated and feared cats until, in the 18th century, a worse enemy than the cat invaded Europe. The brown rat,

multiplying at a terrifying rate, spread disease into every corner of Europe. Even those who thought the cat was the Devil were forced to admit that it was the only protection they had against this more immediate evil.

Cats were again taken on as vermin controllers, and could not be bred fast enough to cope with the demand. They were used to guard homes and businesses, warehouses and food stores – anywhere that rats might invade. Their reputation changed with their success in keeping down the rats. Fortunately for cats, they have never really looked back.

At last, cats – once sacred objects of worship and feared symbols of witchcraft – assumed a more balanced role. They became part of the household, as a hunter and as a pet. Today, the domestic cat is still loved by some and hated by others. Perhaps it is disliked by some people because of its inscrutable independence and apparent indifference to the human race. The cat never really needs its human owner. If necessary the cat can always return to the wild and survive by scavenging and hunting.

Even today, the law does not really protect the cat. In most countries they are still regarded as wild animals as far as the law is concerned. The cat owner does not

need to have a licence for his pet, as a dog owner must, so there is no record of where cats are kept and how. In Britain, if a dog is stolen the thief can be penalized, but there are no such laws about cats. Cats which roam away from home are sometimes stolen for their coats, or sold to laboratories for experiments. Sometimes they are simply ill-treated or neglected by owners who have got bored with looking after them.

Strays roam the streets of many of the world's cities, and bands of domestic cats have reverted to their wild state. These are feral cats. They live as best they can, hiding away from people, and scavenging or hunting for food.

Strays which have little or no human contact may become wild, or feral, after only a generation or two. By that time, they are completely unapproachable, even as kittens. They resemble once again their relatives in the jungle.

The cat family
The cat family, *Felidae*, is divided into three groups. The first group is known as *Felis* (of which the domestic cat is a member). The second group, *Acinonyx*, has claws that cannot be drawn in and out, but are out all the time, like a dog's (the cheetah is the only cat that fits into

this category). Finally, *Panthera* includes cats such as the tiger, leopard and lion; in fact, all the cats which roar. *Felis* can only howl or purr.

All cats are carnivores, or meat eaters. The big cats hunt large vegetable-eating prey such as antelope and zebra. The big cats are the most powerful members of the animal kingdom, and their only real enemy is man. The big cats are hunted for sport or for their skins. Despite protection by law, and the setting up of game reserves, some of these species are now in danger of becoming extinct.

Lions, leopards, cheetahs, the jungle cat, the caracal lynx, and other smaller cats live in Africa and in Asia. The tiger and the snow leopard, and a variety of smaller cats such as the leopard cat, the Chinese desert cat, and the fishing cat, live only in Asia. Few types live only in Africa, but one of the few is the serval, a spotted cat like a small leopard.

The continent of America has a separate collection of wild cats which evolved quite independently. Of these, the ocelot and the margay can be tamed. They have been kept as pets in the United States, though they are not really suitable to live in a family home. Other species include the jaguar, the bobcat, the puma, the pampas cat, and the mountain cat. The northern lynx is the only type which is found in both America and Europe.

A few species of cat roam wild in Europe, and these resemble the domestic cat more than their more powerful big cat relatives. The European wild cat lives

Above: The tiger is a massive and muscular cat which lives in India and South-east Asia. It hunts its prey in jungle and forest, mainly by night. A beautiful animal, with black or brown stripes on a tawny coat, it is also one of the most powerful of the cats and a lethal enemy to many of the smaller animals that share its habitat. *Right:* The Scottish wild cat hides away in the woodland areas of the Scottish Highlands, and is rarely seen. It is untameable, and even tiny orphaned kittens spit and snarl at people and reject any approaches or attempts to feed or look after them. They avoid humans.

in woodland or on high rocky ground. It hunts rodents, birds, rabbits and deer, but is seldom seen and cannot be tamed. It is heavier than the domestic breeds, with a broad, flat head and wide-set ears. Its markings resemble those of a tabby. The lynx species of Europe have the characteristic tufted ears and spotted coats of the lynx group.

The Scottish wild cat, as the name suggests, is found only in Scotland, It belongs to the same group, *Felis Sylvestris*, as the European wild cat and was probably around long before domestic cats were brought into Britain.

Wild cats were found all over Britain until the 19th century when many were shot because they killed game and farm stock. They became more or less extinct, except in the mountains and woodlands of Scotland. Today their numbers are on the increase again.

Chapter two
Choosing a Cat

Whatever your taste, there is a cat to suit you and your purse – longhaired, or shorthaired, exotic or everyday, striped, spotted or plain. But remember, whether you choose a fine pedigree variety or take in a homeless stray, keeping a pet is a responsibility not to be taken lightly.

Before thinking about getting a kitten you must remember that keeping any animal as a pet is a responsibility. It will need warmth and companionship, for all cats and kittens love to be noticed and talked to. It will have to be trained to go outside to be clean, or given a sanitary tray to use indoors. It will have to be fed several times a day when a kitten, and once or twice a day when an adult cat. Feeding can cost quite a lot these days, and to be kept in the best of health and condition, a cat needs a varied diet. It will also need grooming to keep its coat in good condition.

Pedigree or mongrel?
If you feel quite capable of coping with all this, you will probably make a very good cat owner, so the next step is to decide which kind of kitten you prefer. Pedigree kittens are, of course, much more expensive than mongrels.

There are many pedigree varieties to choose from. A pedigree cat has its own birth certificate or pedigree. This means that its parents, grandparents and great-grandparents are known, and that all were of the same type. The cat is then 'pure-bred'.

The pedigree varieties are divided into Longhairs or Persians, and Shorthairs. The Shorthairs are also divided into British, Foreign and Siamese.

Each pedigree variety has a standard by which it can be judged at a show. A hundred points are allocated for such a standard, which sets out the characteristics – that is, the body and head shape, eyes, tail and condition – which would make up the perfect cat. The points are allocated according to the importance placed on the various characteristics required.

Whether you choose a pedigree or a mongrel kitten, it will need careful attention when you get it home. A little butter on the paws makes the kitten settle down to lick it off.

Choosing a longhaired cat
The Longhairs or Persians all have much the same head, body shape and tail length. The heads are broad and round, with short broad noses, the ears small, the eyes big and round, and the bodies cobby on short sturdy legs. The tails are short and very fluffy. The fur is long and flowing. The colours include the Whites, which have beautiful soft and silky coats. Their eyes may be orange, blue, or even odd-eyed, which means that one eye is orange and the other blue.

The Blacks have jet black fur and beautiful copper-coloured eyes. The Blues, most popular of all the longhairs, have very long fur and deep orange eyes. Red Selfs have rich red coats and large copper eyes. The Creams have creamy-yellow coats, while Blue-Creams, a female-only variety, has the fur of the two colours softly intermingled for the British standard, but with cream and blue patches in the American standard. The Smokes, often called the cats of contrasts because their undercoats are white, have

Top: This kitten feels safe and at home in the sleeping quarters provided for it.
Above: Young kittens arrive at the Animal Welfare Society's headquarters. The Society will try to find homes for them with people who will look after them well.

top coats of black or blue. Then there are the very popular Tabbies, which all have the same pattern of markings. The Brown has dense black markings; the Silver has pale silver fur with black markings; and the Red has rich red fur and even deeper red markings.

In addition, there are two female-only varieties, the Tortoiseshells with patched fur of black, red and cream, and the Tortoiseshell and Whites which have the same coloured patching with the addition of white. Males are born very occasionally, but are usually unable to sire kittens.

Another very popular variety are the Chinchillas, with their long white fur delicately tipped with black, and their beautiful sea-green eyes.

Very striking cats are the Bi-Colours, which have long coats of two colours. They can be white with black; white with blue; white with red; and white with cream. The two colours should be absolutely distinct from one another.

The attractive Colourpoints, known as Himalayans in the States, are most unusual because their coats are similar to those of the Siamese – the body fur is pale, but the face, ears, legs and tails are dark. The eyes are blue, and the head and body shapes are the same as in the other Longhairs.

Two varieties differ from the other cats with long fur. In fact, they are more like the Angoras, the first longhaired cats in Europe, which appeared in the 16th century. The heads are not so round, the ears are a little larger, and the bodies and tails longer. The coats are not so luxurious. One such is the Birman which has similar colouring to the Colourpoints, but with the unusual feature of four white feet like gloves, the back ones coming to a point up the hind legs. The other is the Turkish, which really did come from Turkey to Britain in the 1960s. It is white, with red ears and a red-ringed tail. Turkish cats are particularly unusual because they like swimming in warm rivers and pools. The fur is not nearly so long as many other longhairs.

Maine Coons are not known in Britain, but have been bred in the United States for over a hundred years. They originated from the mating of the resident shorthaired cats in Maine and longhaired cats taken there by sailors. These massive cats were called Coon because their fur is like that of the raccoon. They were said to have been bred from cat/raccoon matings, but this is not possible. Maine Coons have full silky fur, medium heads with large ears, large eyes, and muscular bodies on strong legs, with long, tapering tails. The first Maines were Tabbies with white chests, but now most colours are recognized. They are gentle, intelligent cats which make wonderful pets as they are very affectionate and easy to handle.

Most Longhairs are of a quieter disposition than some other varieties, such as the Siamese. They are quite happy to be the only cat in the household, loving to be fussed over and talked to. They are intelligent, playful, and make most decorative companions. Many are excellent rat and mouse catchers, but are not as inclined to go after birds as some other cats.

British shorthaired cats

There are three kinds of shorthaired cats, the British, the Foreign and the Siamese. The British shorthairs are the pedigree descendants of the cats that first arrived

in Britain in Roman times, and they come in several colours and patterns.

The British shorthairs are similar in build to the Longhairs or Persians, and are very sturdy and strong-looking cats. They have broad, round heads, with full cheeks, small ears, short, straight noses, and large, round eyes. Their tails are thick at the base with rounded tips, and are shortish. The coats are short and very dense. The colours available are very similar to those of the Longhairs. There are three Whites with different eye colourings; the Blacks with shining jet black fur; the British Blues with even coloured coats, the most popular variety of the British cats; and the very rare Creams. There are the Tabbies, with the same markings as the longhaired, though it is also possible to have Tabbies with mackerel markings, said to resemble those of the fish. The coat has numerous narrow lines running from the spine. The colours are red, brown and silver.

Tortoiseshells and Tortoiseshell and

Whites both have patched coats and are female-only varieties. There are also female-only Blue Creams, produced by mating Blues and Creams together. A very old variety, which seemed to have disappeared altogether for some years, but has now reappeared and is being bred in a number of colours, is the Spotted shorthair. Its characteristics are exactly the same as for the other British cats, but the coat should be highly spotted with the spotting distinct from the background fur.

Silver with black spots is very popular. Red with deep red spots is also very appealing, and Brown with black spots is

Right: Two Persian kittens take a first look at their new home. Fluffy kittens like this will need a lot of attention to keep their coats in good condition. *Below:* This attractive little longhaired kitten has been carefully groomed and looks the picture of health. Though so young, it is alert and ready for a game.

Types of coat patterns

Though many millions of cats the world over have patterned coats, nearly all the markings seem different. Among the pedigree shorthairs, however, some varieties are required to have a definite pattern or type of marking. Even some of these may vary slightly from one cat to another.

ticked

Each hair has bands of a darker colour

mackerel

Narrow lines run vertically from the spine, like the markings of a fish.

spotted

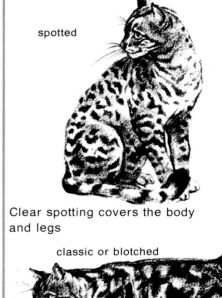

Clear spotting covers the body and legs

classic or blotched

Defined markings, with a letter 'M' on the forehead.

in ready demand, particularly as a pet cat.

A fairly new variety is the Bi-Colour, whose colourings can be similar to those of the Longhairs. They are comparatively rare, but a few may be seen at the shows. It is also possible to have shorthaired Smokes, with pale silver undercoats, and black or blue top fur. Although the contrasts may not be quite so distinctive as that of the longhaired varieties, they are very pretty cats.

Another new variety is the British Tipped. These again have the same characteristics as the other British types, but the coat is different. The undercoat is white, and the tips of each hair are delicately marked with black, red, brown,

chocolate or lilac. Of course, the tipping must be the same colour all over, and must be evenly distributed giving an almost sparkling effect to the fur.

There is one cat that can never be mistaken for any other variety. This is the Manx, which should have no tail at all. There should be a decided hollow where the tails start in other cats. Manx cats are said to have descended from cats that swam ashore to the Isle of Man from a wrecked galleon in the Spanish Armada. The noses of Manx cats are a little longer than in other British varieties, and the ears are slightly pointed. Their walk is referred to as a 'rabbity' gait, because they have no tail and rather long back

This sturdy Chinchilla litter is nearly old enough to leave the mother. The kittens are all much the same size and there is no weak one. Pedigree kittens should be about twelve weeks old when they go to their new homes. They should also be fully weaned and house-trained. A diet sheet should be supplied.

legs. Any colour or coat pattern is recognized. Manx are difficult to breed to order, because Manx cats can have kittens with tails, kittens with short tails, called Stumpies, as well as the true tailless Manx. Because they are so different from other cats, Manx cats are popular as pets, particularly in the United States.

16

Left: An alert Sealpoint Siamese, with good coloured ears, mask and legs. Siamese are the most popular shorthaired variety. They are demanding, need to be noticed, and frequently require constant attention from their owners. But they make excellent companions because they are very talkative by nature. *Right:* This little tabby kitten appears to be lost in the jungle — or so he thinks. A new kitten should only be allowed out in the garden under supervision. It may stray until it has settled down and got its bearings.

The Russian Blues may have come from Archangel in Russia aboard ships, but careful breeding has produced the very beautiful cats seen at shows today. They have short shining fur, clear blue in colour, but with a silvery sheen. The heads are short and wedge-shaped with large, pointed ears, and the vivid green eyes are almond in shape. Their bodies are long and graceful on tall legs, and the tails fairly long and tapering.

Russian Blues are quiet in character and in voice, and can live happily in flats and apartments, loving to be close to their owners but not demanding too much attention.

Abyssinians differ from the other Foreign varieties in that the short fine fur is ticked with darker colourings. The coats may be rich golden brown or a lustrous copper red. Their heads are broad, tapering to a firm wedge, but not sharply pointed. The comparatively large ears should be tufted, and the large bright eyes may be amber, hazel or green in colour. The bodies are of medium length, with fairly long and tapering tails.

Most Abyssinians are light-coloured, almost white, around the lips and lower jaws, but if this extends down the neck it is a fault, as are white lockets. A broken necklet – that is a dark line like a necklace – is allowed, but it must not go completely around the neck.

It is also possible to have an Abyssinian with blue-grey fur ticked with a deep steel blue. This is a very old variety which is still fairly rare, but Abyssinians are favourites as pets, because they love company, are very friendly, and make ideal companions. They are quiet and easy to train to walk on leads. However, they dislike being kept in confinement.

Burmese cats were introduced into Britain from America and they are now a very popular variety. Their numbers and colourings have increased so much over the years that they have their own show, and they are rapidly overtaking the Siamese. Those seen in the United States have rounder heads and slightly cobbier bodies than those bred in Britain.

In Britain the heads should be a little rounded on top, tapering to short, blunt wedges. The head is not so long as that of the Siamese. The ears should be medium in size, and the large lustrous eyes may be any shade of yellow. The bodies should be of medium length, the legs slender and the straight tails of medium length.

In the States, the Burmese are Brown, but in Britain the colours vary and include the Brown, Blue, Chocolate, Lilac, Red, Cream, Brown Tortie (or tortoiseshell), Blue Tortie, Chocolate Tortie, or Lilac Tortie. The coats should be very short and fine, with a satin-like sheen.

Burmese cats have distinct personalities, and early training is essential if they are not to rule the household. They do make delightful companions; they are very affectionate and intelligent, and like to go everywhere with their owner if they can.

Havanas are graceful cats, similar to Siamese, with their long, lithe bodies, on slim, dainty legs, and long, whipped tails. The heads are long, the ears large, and

the oriental shaped eyes a deep green. The American Havanas have shorter heads and medium-length fur, whereas in Britain the fur should be short, fine and glossy, and a rich chestnut-brown colour. They are gentle, home-loving cats, quiet in character, and very intelligent.

Very similar in type are the Foreign Lilacs, which have frosty-grey fur, and definite green eyes. Another variety with the same type and shape are the Foreign Whites, with gleaming white silky fur, and clear brilliant blue, almond eyes.

The Foreign Blacks have the same characteristics, with long heads and large ears. The fur is a shining jet-black, and the oriental eyes a beautiful green.

It is also possible to have Foreign Smokes, with similar heads and body shape, but with pale, silvery coloured undercoats, and top fur of black, blue, chocolate, lilac, red, cream, or even tortoiseshell.

In Britain there are cats like the Foreign Lilacs, Blacks and Whites but with patterned coats that are distinctively spotted, and scarab markings on the heads. These are known as the Oriental

Spotted Tabbies. The colours may be brown with black spotting, blue spots on beige, chocolate spotting on bronze, lilac spots on beige, red spotting on apricot, and rich cream on pale cream. The fur is short, fine and glossy. These cats have been produced by careful breeding.

The Egyptian Mau, bred in the United States, is similar. The heads are slightly rounded but the bodies not quite so long. There are three colours: the Silver with charcoal markings, the Bronze, with dark brown markings and the Smoke with charcoal spots.

All the Foreign shorthair coats look good after hard hand grooming from head to tail. Rubbing all over with a piece of velvet, a silk handkerchief or scarf or a chamois leather is the best way to make the coat really shine.

The Korats are very rare cats imported into the United States from Thailand, which may now be seen in small numbers in Britain. They are unusual in that their faces are heart-shaped, the heads small with large ears; the eyes green, and the bodies and tails are medium in length. The distinctive fur is silver-blue in colour, and tipped with silver. They are happy, friendly cats and are said to have sweet and loving natures.

If you prefer a shorthaired cat that is very unusual in appearance and needs very little grooming, you could choose a Rex. These cats, sometimes referred to as poodle cats, have wavy or curly coats, There are two kinds, the Cornish and the Devon. Both appeared in the west of England, the Cornish in 1950 and the Devon in 1960.

The change in the coats from that of other cats was caused by mutations. A mutation is a sudden variation which may appear in an animal for no apparent reason. By careful breeding it was found possible to produce kittens with similar coats, but the two varieties did not mix, so it was no use mating one kind to the other.

The Cornish have short plush coats which curl, wave or ripple – even the whiskers and eyebrows are crinkled. The heads are short and wedged in shape, with large ears covered with fine fur, and with straight noses. The Devon Rex have very short and fine fur, soft and wavy, and the heads are wedge-shaped with full cheeks and large ears. The noses have a definite stop or bend in the middle. Both cats have real personalities and are full of character, loving to be noticed, highly intelligent, and showing affection willingly.

Although it has no tail, the Manx cat still has a good sense of balance. It can walk on narrow ledges or branches, or climb trees without any difficulty.

The Devon are said to have a wicked sense of humour that goes well with their elfin looks.

Rex cats can be any colour. Of all the cats they are the easiest to groom, as they do not moult regularly. Hard hand-grooming should keep them looking spick and span, with the occasional comb through with a small-toothed metal comb to remove any dust or fleas.

The elegant and popular Siamese have Foreign characteristics, but are not usually classified with the Foreign varieties. Those now seen in Britain, the United States and many other parts of the world have descended from a pair that came from the Royal Palace in Bangkok. There are now thousands in Britain alone, but it is said that they are rarely seen in Thailand nowadays. At first the kittens were very delicate and hard to rear, but careful breeding now produces Siamese that are as healthy as any other varieties.

They are exotic in appearance, with light coloured bodies and dark faces (masks), ears, legs and tails, known as the points. The heads are long, with large ears, the bodies long and svelte on slim legs, the tails long and tapering. They have beautiful deep-blue, almond-shaped eyes.

The original Siamese cats were the Seal-points, which have cream bodies and seal brown points, but many other points colourings have now been bred. These include the Blue-points, with glacial white body colourings and blue points; the Chocolate with ivory body and milk chocolate points; the Lilacs, originally known in the States as the Frost points, with magnolia body and lilac points; the Tabby-points with pale bodies and varying tabby-coloured points; the Red-points with white body and bright reddish-gold points; the female-only Tortie-points with patched points of various colours, including blue, chocolate or lilac, with some red or cream markings included. There are also Cream-points, with whitish cream bodies and deeper cream points. It is also possible to breed a number of other mixed points colourings.

In the United States the Tabby-points, the Cream, the Red and the Tortie-points are known as the Colourpoint Shorthairs. This is because other cats have been used in the original breeding and so they are considered to be hybrids, which means that their breeding is not pure for the necessary number of generations required in America.

Balinese cats were first born in Siamese litters but their fur was fluffy and silky, rather than short, and their tails were fluffy too. They are now being bred in the United States and in Britain, with characteristics and colours as for the Siamese.

Non-pedigree cats
A mongrel is a cat whose parentage and forebears are unknown. Naturally, they have ancestors. In fact, it is from their ancestors that, by selective breeding, all the pedigree shorthaired cats were produced. It was not until the first cat show was held in 1871 that anyone thought of keeping records and so eventually producing pedigrees. Indiscriminate breeding over the centuries has produced mongrels in hundreds of colours and coat patterns. The vast majority have some form of tabby markings, frequently with white on their fur. All colours are possible and the mongrel kittens can be most attractive and highly intelligent. They are usually very healthy and sturdy. They tend to mature earlier than many of the pedigree varieties, and are very self-reliant. As neutered pets they make excellent and very affectionate companions.

There are also cross-bred cats resulting from two entirely different pedigree cats being mated together, or from matings between one pedigree parent and a mongrel. Such kittens are usually very attractive, but there are few about, as

Maine Coons are said to be one of the oldest varieties in the United States. At one time, cat shows were held in Maine just for them. They are still a very popular breed.

Above: A farmyard cat with her kittens. Most farms have many cats to keep down the vermin, and mixed matings produce beautiful kittens of all colours and coat patterns. In the past, such kittens have been used to start breeding new pedigree varieties. *Left:* A beautiful White Devon Rex with the typical wavy coat of the breed. The first Devon Rex was found in Devon, running wild on the moors. It is possible that it was the result of a mutation that appeared suddenly in cats from farms. Careful breeding was necessary to produce cats that all had wavy fur. New coat colours were produced by cross mating. *Right:* Feral cats living wild. These are not related in any way to the European wild cat, but are cats that may be strays or unwanted. They may breed in fields, in caves and forests, thus becoming semi-wild and very difficult to tame.

naturally breeders guard their pedigree stock carefully to see that they do not get out and mismate with mongrels.

Finding the right kitten

The best way to find out about pedigree kittens and to see the various kinds is to visit a cat show and meet the breeders. The show catalogues carry advertisements of breeders throughout the country. There are many cat shows held over a year, sometimes in conjunction with local agricultural shows. Some daily and evening newspapers, and local papers may have advertisements. A reputable pet shop will often recommend breeders. It is always best to visit the breeder's home and see the litter if you can. You will be able to see the mother and also the conditions under which the animals are kept.

If you want to go in for breeding it is as well to buy the best cat you can afford. She should have a good pedigree and be of good type, and when she is adult she should be mated with an equally good male.

If you are not intending to breed, a pedigree kitten that is not quite up to show standard should be slightly less expensive than one that is.

If finding a mongrel kitten proves difficult, the local branches of animal welfare societies usually have cats and kittens wanting good homes, or the names and addresses of people whose cats have had kittens. Do not be surprised if the animal society ask to inspect your home. They want to be sure that the cat or kitten will be happy with you and well looked after.

You may hear that a neighbour's cat has just had kittens, and be able to go and choose the one you like best. There may be advertisements on local notice boards too. Pet shops sometimes have mongrel litters, but do be sure that the shop is of good repute, and that the kittens are very lively and playful.

You may care to consider taking a cat, rather than a kitten, from one of the animal welfare societies. It is well worth while doing this, as you may be able to adopt a cat whose owner has died or one whose family have had to move into a flat where no pets are allowed. Such a cat may take a little longer to settle down, but in a very short while will really show appreciation and readily give affection.

A cat that has been a stray may be a little apprehensive and unsure of itself at first, and patience will be needed until it becomes used to the fact that it is really wanted again by a new owner.

All cats and kittens that come from one of the animal societies will be examined by a veterinary surgeon to make sure that they are in the best of health before going to a new home.

Whatever kitten you choose, be sure to select the one that looks the healthiest and most full of life. Make sure its coat is not clinging to the sides of its body and that its eyes are bright and clean in the corners. It should not have a running nose and inside the ears should look clean. There should be no signs of messiness under the tail or fleas in the fur. The kitten should feel solid to the touch; the stomach should not be swollen or the backbone easily felt. The fur should look well groomed and the tail be held high.

A mongrel kitten should be about eight to nine weeks old, and a pedigree kitten should be about twelve weeks. At that age it should be fully weaned with a full set of milk teeth. Watch the kitten run and play to see that it is steady on its legs and is not easily frightened.

If you are buying a pedigree, tell the breeder if it is to be used for breeding or is to be a pet only. Ask the breeder to tell you the good and bad points, so that you know a little about the variety even if you are not using the cat for breeding. Before bringing the kitten home, check whether it has been wormed and vaccinated against Feline Infectious Enteritis (FIE).

Chapter three
Bringing a Kitten Home

There is nothing more enchanting than a young kitten taking its first exploratory steps in its new home. A kitten needs care, but not over-fussing, to grow into a contented cat.

A small kitten that has just left its mother will find life rather strange at first. Its feelings will be mixed – curiosity about its new surroundings may be mingled with fear and apprehension, and perhaps loneliness when it suddenly finds itself separated from its family.

But kittens are naturally sociable and inquisitive creatures, and it is up to the owner to make sure that a young kitten is settled into its new home as easily and as quickly as possible.

The kitten's equipment

Once you have chosen your kitten and know when you can go to collect it, you can start getting together the things it will need. Even if you buy a kitten from a pet shop or get one from a welfare society, you should buy the equipment you will need to look after it as soon as possible.

The first requirement for a young kitten is a comfortable bed. There are several types of beds and baskets on the market, but it is quite easy to make a small bed yourself. The kitten will prefer to sleep in something small and enclosing, rather than a full-sized cat bed anyway, and would soon grow out of a kitten-sized bed.

All you need is a small cardboard box, with the front cut down so that the kitten can step in and out. Line the box with newspaper and then plenty of warm bedding – old woollies or a blanket are ideal. This way, you have a disposable bed, and can just throw it away if it gets soiled.

If you do want to buy a bed straightaway, two points should be borne in mind. Firstly, make sure that the bed is easy to clean; a plain wicker basket is better than the types lined with fabric. The basket can be filled with plenty of

A kitten that has just left its mother will find life a bit lonely at first. It should be made a fuss of when it first arrives, so that it feels at home and secure in its new surroundings.

bedding and a cushion to make a nest for the kitten.

The other point to remember is that when the kitten grows into a cat, it may have its own views about where it is going to sleep, and the smart and expensive bed you have bought may not be its choice. Some cats prefer to sleep on a chair or on the floor, or on the most uncomfortable looking ledges. You may be able to save yourself trouble and expense by waiting to see whether your cat has strong preferences before you buy a bed.

The kitten will also need its own dishes for food, milk and water. Dishes for a young kitten should be shallow and firm-standing. You can use saucers, but they tip up easily if a paw is put on the side. Flat-bottomed dishes are better – certainly for milk and water. You can buy heavy pottery dishes, or cheaper plastic ones which are quite adequate. Cats find it easier to lap milk or water from a broad, shallow dish than from a deep bowl.

Contrary to popular belief, cats drink water, not milk, to quench their thirst. Milk is a food and some cats do not like it much when they get past kittenhood, as they find it indigestible. So a bowl of fresh water must always be placed near the kitten's food.

Never use family dishes for the cat's food, and always wash the cat's dishes thoroughly after each meal.

The kitten will have to stay indoors at first, so it must be provided with a sanitary tray. Both the shallow plastic tray and the litter to go in it are sold in pet shops. There must be enough litter in the tray for the kitten to dig, and it must be changed frequently. A kitten will not use a dirty tray, and may get into the habit of using corners of the house instead.

The tray should be set on a piece of newspaper in a permanent position, so that the kitten knows where it is. The tray itself can be washed when necessary.

You can also buy or make a selection of simple toys for the kitten to play with.

Water is an essential part of a cat's diet. Providing milk for your kitten or cat is not enough, because milk is a food rather than a drink. Cats need a bowl of fresh water each day.

Avoid anything with sharp edges or bits that can be bitten off and swallowed – a ball and a cloth mouse are popular starters, and lots of toys can be made or improvised (see Chapter 4).

The last essential, if you want to protect the household furniture, is a scratching post. Cats cannot resist stropping their claws and this behaviour is instinctive. Even if they are outdoor cats, they often seem to wait until they are indoors to do their sharpening act. The only way round having the furniture ruined is to provide a special post for the kitten to scratch its claws on, and then train it to use this and no other.

Scratching posts can be bought or made. A log or plank of wood will do, provided it is firmly anchored to a base so that it will not move around when the cat uses it. Or you can buy various kinds of scratching posts and panels from a pet shop.

Collecting the kitten

Now you are ready for the kitten's arrival. When you go to collect it, take a strong carrier with you. If you don't want to invest in a travelling basket (see page 59) straightaway, you can buy cardboard carriers, specially designed for cats, from the pet shop. But these may not be substantial enough as the cat gets bigger, and you will need a carrier for visits to the vet and other journeys, so it is worth buying something that is fairly strong.

The carrier should obviously have some ventilation holes in it, and some types even have built-in windows so that the cat can see out.

The kitten will probably object quite strongly to being put into the carrier. It will not have come into contact with such a thing before, during its early days with mother and family, and so may find the new experience surprising. Make sure that the carrier is lined with plenty of newspaper, and once the kitten is in, on no account let it out until you get home. There are bound to be protesting wails on the journey, but this is quite normal, and sympathy should never make you open the carrier. A terrified kitten leaping out and making a dash for it will not be easy to catch.

Settling in

When you get home, it is best to confine the kitten to one room for its first venture out of the carrier. For one thing, it will be easier to track it down if it decides to make off back to its mother, and for another it will be less awe-inspiring for the kitten. Allow it to wander around for a while, exploring. Keep an eye on it at this stage, and make sure that there are no dangers for it – places it can get stuck in or behind, or an open fire. The tiny kitten has little or no experience of life and its hazards, and will have to learn what to avoid. But at this age, it is up to the new owner to see that all is well.

When the kitten has had a chance to look around for a while, show it where its things are. Ideally, its bed and tray should be together, and it can be fed in the same place too. This way, it knows exactly which is its own domain and can retire there for rest and a sense of security.

The first meals

Give the kitten a small introductory snack. Kittens have very small stomachs and need to be fed small meals about four or five times a day. Start as you mean to go on by establishing which the main meal times are going to be when the cat is older. For example, if it suits the family routine to feed the cat a big meal in the morning and a small one in the evening, try to establish this routine from the start by giving the kitten its two meat meals morning and evening, gradually increasing the size of the morning one as the other meals are cut out. The kitten's other meals during these early days should be milk-based.

Some of the canned cat foods are too rich for a young kitten, but those without liver are suitable and should not upset the kitten's stomach. Tinned cat foods have the advantage of being balanced to include all the nutrients a cat needs for healthy growth. A diet of, say, raw meat alone may lack some essentials.

The kitten could have a small meat meal – canned food, or cooked or raw mince – in the morning, and milk or milk and a solid food such as baby cereal at lunchtime. Then it could have this same

The right way to hold a kitten
A young kitten has a very small and delicate body which can be damaged by rough handling. It is very important that it is picked up and held properly, so that body and paws are supported. If it is grabbed and clutched in the wrong way, its bones and muscles may be harmed. Or it may object to such treatment and turn on its owner, scratching to be set free.

The right way: Let the kitten sit on one of your hands, so that you are supporting its back legs. Support the front paws with the other hand.

The wrong way: Never pick up a kitten by the scruff of its neck. Only the mother cat knows how to do this. You may damage the muscles in the neck.

The wrong way: Never leave the body unsupported like this. The body is stretched and forms a dead weight.

pair of meals at teatime and later on in the evening. As the kitten grows up, you can cut out the milk meals and make the other two meals bigger. Some people cut down to only one meal a day when the cat is adult, but many cats prefer a main meal and a snack throughout their lives.

You will soon be able to gauge how much to give a small kitten. On the one hand, its stomach is tiny and delicate. On the other hand, it will grow very fast and really needs to be given as much as it can eat while it is growing up. As a rough guide, a kitten of eight to ten weeks needs 4 or 5 oz (112–140 g) of food a day.

You can buy vitamin and mineral supplements from the pet shop, and these are specially designed for cats. But if the kitten is having a balanced diet, it should not need further supplements. Some people feel, however, that the extra

nutrition for a growing kitten is a good idea which should be encouraged.

As the kitten grows older, the diet can become more varied, and the types of food will be dealt with in more detail in the next chapter. But what you feed your cat is, in the end, between you and your cat. It will have quite definite preferences as it grows up. The first meal in its new home is mainly to make the kitten feel welcome and established. It knows then that, despite its strange new surroundings, food, at least, will be provided. You should make a fuss of the kitten during this early period. It will feel lonely and strange, and will require plenty of care until it has settled down.

After a fairly short time, the kitten will probably feel tired and want to go to sleep. Small kittens tire very easily – one moment they are dancing around after a ball, and the next minute they are

Above: This cat has a surprisingly brave companion during its meal. *Right:* A cat should have its own feeding dishes, and not be given food from the family plates. The best sort of dishes are flat and shallow with a broad base so that they cannot be tipped over easily. Saucers can be used for small kittens, but they are not very stable, particularly if the kitten tries to get too close to its meal and puts a paw on the side overturning the saucer and its contents.

fast asleep.

Do not disturb the kitten when it has settled into its bed. Keep other people from fussing over it until it wakes up.

A careful welcoming and settling-in ritual should ensure that the kitten quickly feels secure in its new surroundings, and it should then cause no problems. A kitten that is just brought

home and dumped to fend for itself may be more trouble in the long run, as it will feel anguished and cry for its mother, driving the whole household mad with its surprisingly loud and plaintive wails.

Early training

The most essential early lesson for the kitten is house-training, if this has not already been taken care of by the original owner. Cats are basically clean animals and house training should not be difficult, provided the kitten does not get into sloppy ways. After each meal, put it into its tray. If it seems bewildered at first,

keep putting it into the tray until it uses it. Once it has used it, it will know that this is the right place. The mother cat teaches her kittens to dig a hole in the earth, and a kitten of this age automatically starts to dig and bury. So remember to put a reasonable layer of litter in the tray to make digging possible.

If the kitten makes a mess anywhere in the house, and you are around at the time, speak to it sharply and take it straight to the tray. Don't hit the kitten, shout at it or rub its nose in the mess. It will just be afraid and not understand what is going on. There are bound to be

A young kitten needs lots of sleep and should be provided with a comfortable bed. You can make one yourself, or buy one from a pet shop. *Above:* This type of bed is cosy for a kitten. The back and roof keep out draughts, and the front is low enough for the kitten to climb in and out. The bed is made of wicker so it can be cleaned easily. A soft blanket makes ideal bedding as it gives the kitten additional warmth and comfort. *Right:* Another wicker bed, bought for growing into. A blanket makes a warm nest to curl up in and prevents the kitten feeling that it is too small for its surroundings.

a few misinterpretations of the house rules to start with but, so long as you are firm when these happen, the kitten will learn quickly.

When you clean up after the kitten on these occasions, make sure that you scrub the carpet or surface to remove all trace of the smell. If it can smell the place, the kitten will use the same spot again.

If you are not there and discover the accident later, there is no point in scolding the kitten. It will have forgotten the incident and so will not understand why you are annoyed. When this happens all you can do is to clean up thoroughly.

Another essential to get into the kitten's mind as quickly as possible is that scratching the furniture is forbidden. The scratching post has already been mentioned, but it is not easy to get a kitten to use one. House training is easy because the kitten instinctively feels it is right to be clean. Unfortunately, it does not have the same instincts about not ruining brand new chair covers.

As soon as the kitten starts to strop its claws on some forbidden area, pick it up and take it to the scratching post. Place its front paws on the post and move them up and down to imitate scratching. The first few times you do this, the kitten will probably just look contemptuous and go back to scratching the carpet, but if

Above: It is natural for cats and kittens to sharpen their claws. A tree trunk in the garden makes a useful scratching post and stops it from clawing the furniture.

Introducing other pets

If there are other pets, such as a dog or another cat, the new kitten should be introduced to them gradually. A fully grown cat may be jealous of the intruder if it has been used to being the sole family cat. But it can be made to get used to the idea.

Introduce the two to one another and stand guard over them. They may spit at one another to begin with. If they do, separate them and make a fuss of each one individually. The new kitten will probably get used to the situation first, and will be ready to play. After a time, both cats can be taught to be friends. Never leave them alone together while there is still antagonism, and be ready to go to the rescue if the older cat shows signs of attacking the little one. Keep them in separate rooms until you feel

Right: Cats and dogs must be introduced to one another properly so that neither one becomes jealous of the other. *Below:* As soon as a kitten is old enough it must be vaccinated against Feline Infectious Enteritis. It is not safe to let it mix with other cats till this has been done.

Above: Kittens and indoor cats should be provided with a sanitary tray filled with litter. The litter should be deep enough for the cat to dig, and it should be changed frequently. In order to house train the kitten properly, it should be put into the tray after every meal.

you are painstaking and firm enough, you should be able to get the message through.

Once the kitten can go outside (if you have a garden it can use) it should get into the habit of stropping its claws on tree trunks and branches, though it will still want to strop indoors too. Cats in the wild instinctively use wood with bark on it to scratch, so a wooden scratching post is the most acceptable type for the kitten to use.

You may have to leave a tiny kitten alone in the house – for example, if you only have one kitten and you have to go out for any length of time. Until it is used to the layout of the house, and until you are sure that it is reliably house-trained, it is best to keep it confined to one room on these occasions. It can be left with its bed, tray and some toys for a few hours. But it should be remembered that young kittens do get lonely if left alone too much. If everyone in the family is out at work or school all day, it is kinder to have two kittens so that they can keep one another company. Or there may already be another pet in the house, which would be company for the kitten.

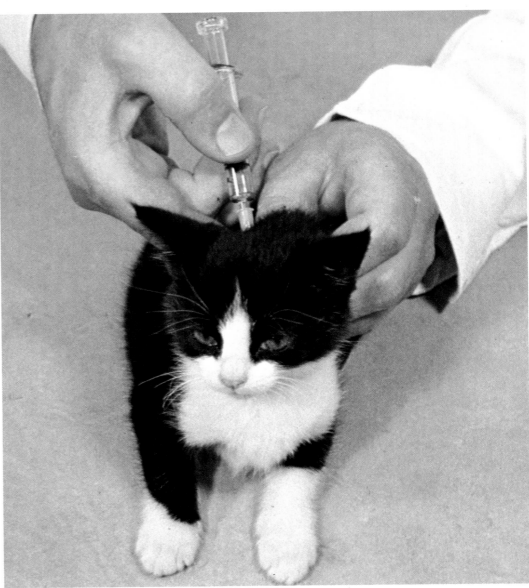

Left: Life is full of surprises for a young kitten out exploring. But the guinea pig is part of the family, so the two animals have to learn to live with one another. *Right:* Even small kittens try to communicate with their owners. This kitten has an urgent message. Its ears are pricked and it looks up intently, trying to convey what it wants.

sure that there will be no more problems. Once it has got used to the idea, even the family cat will no doubt appreciate a new and lively companion.

The situation is much the same if you have a dog. Cats and dogs traditionally do not get on, but if they belong to the same household they can become inseparable companions. However, the early days need careful handling. Keep feeding times and places strictly separate, and keep the animals separate too. The dog will not be above eating the kitten's meal as well as its own if things are not kept under control.

Dogs instinctively attack cats, too, so be ready to intervene if there is growling and spitting at the first few meetings. Do not let the dog chase the cat. If the dog is assured (by being made a fuss of) that its own position in the household is not going to change, it will accept the new playmate.

The kitten and young children
Young children must also be taught how to treat a small kitten – or a fully grown cat, for that matter. A kitten has delicate bones that cannot take a lot of rough handling, and young children do sometimes get over-enthusiastic and grab the kitten roughly, or clasp it too tightly. The kitten may then retaliate by scratching the child But if a small child is taught to be gentle and pick up the kitten properly, an inseparable bond can develop between the two.

If there is a young baby in the house, hygiene is the main thing to watch. For example, the baby may crawl up to the cat's dishes and eat its meal – and vice versa. The sanitary tray should obviously be kept well out of the baby's reach.

Cats and kittens like to snuggle up to people, so the cat should never be allowed near where the baby is sleeping. It might smother the baby by lying on its face. Any tendency to bad temper and scratching must be watched for, too. Some cats – though not many – cannot learn to get on with young children and might hurt them when angry.

Taking the kitten to the vet
Soon after the kitten arrives, when it has had a chance to settle in, it should be taken for a check-up and vaccination by the veterinary surgeon.

All kittens must be vaccinated against Feline Infectious Enteritis, a fatal disease for cats (see page 61). This is normally done at ten to twelve weeks of age. If you have bought a pedigree kitten that stayed with its mother until it was twelve weeks old, it will probably have been vaccinated by the time you get it. A mongrel cat, which leaves its mother earlier, probably will not have been. If you discover from the original owner of the litter that the kitten has not been vaccinated, check with your vet about the precise age, and take the kitten along.

At the same time, the vet will give the kitten a check-up to make sure that it is starting off in good health. The kitten will probably have been wormed before it left its first home, but the vet will probably give it a second worming tablet. He will check the coat for any signs of fleas, and the ears for early signs of infection or parasites. He will also look at the eyes and inside the mouth.

The vet will then give you a certificate to state that the cat has been vaccinated. He will also give you the date for the next vaccination, or booster. This may be one or two years later. The certificate should be kept in a safe place. You will

need it if you have to leave the cat in a boarding cattery, and it will also remind you when the booster is due.

Playing and climbing
Small kittens need a lot of sleep, so they should not be disturbed when they suddenly curl up in the middle of a game. Young children sometimes forget this if they want to go on playing with the kitten, but it will soon be awake again and ready for another game.

After its initial wariness, a kitten quickly settles down and becomes sociable with its new owner. Unfortunately, this sociability can involve a lot of climbing and rushing around, a phase of the kitten's life which is short, but exhausting for the owners! Try to discourage the habit of running up people's clothes on to their shoulders. This may seem endearing in a tiny kitten, but can be a painful experience when the animal has sharp claws and weighs several pounds. Some kittens climb up curtains, bookshelves and anything else they can find, and this too can spoil fabrics. Cats are very delicate in their movements, though, and rarely break ornaments. Even from a very young age, they seem to be able to pick their way through a densely covered area without displacing a single thing.

The best way to discourage the kitten from doing all the things it should not, is to make sure that it has plenty of toys to keep it occupied. Try to devote some time each day to playing with it. Boredom is a prime cause of a cat getting into mischief.

Be careful, also, that the kitten cannot climb up and get out of windows when your back is turned.

Some cats never go outside if their owners live in flats or busy urban areas. But if you have a garden and propose to let the kitten use it, introduce it to this new environment gradually. A kitten must never be allowed to mix with other cats until it has been vaccinated against Feline Infectious Enteritis, so it must be kept indoors until then.

After this, only let it out under supervision to explore a small area at a time. There are many hazards for an inexperienced kitten out of doors, not the least of which is traffic.

Chapter four
The Kitten Grows Up

A kitten should be trained so that as it grows up it will fit into the household routine. Regular meals, somewhere to sharpen its claws and a secure place to sleep are vital factors in a cat's life.

When it is ready to leave its mother, a kitten is a round, fluffy creature which grows into a gangly adolescent before becoming a fully grown cat at about 18 months old. During its kittenhood and adolescence, it is playful and inquisitive, though its interest in toys will gradually diminish as it grows up. Nevertheless, some cats happily chase a ball or suddenly pounce at an imaginary mouse at quite a sedate age.

A kitten that is given plenty of attention and playtime from its early days is more likely to grow into an intelligent, lively and aware cat than one which is left completely to its own devices. Play not only helps to develop strong muscles, but it also trains the kitten's eye and reactions, and makes it more alert to human companionship.

Making toys

Toys need not be elaborate. In fact, a screwed-up paper bag gradually unfolding is of far more interest to an inquisitive mind than many of the more static toys you can buy.

Kittens will play quite happily alone, though they do appreciate some games, such as someone throwing a ball to chase, or swinging a toy mouse on a string to jump up at. They enjoy anything that involves climbing, pouncing, jumping and swinging. An empty cardboard box makes an excellent cave for imaginary exploration and a bed with a counterpane down to the ground becomes a secret grotto where a kitten can lie in wait to pounce at anyone who happens to pass

Left: If your cat tends to roam, you can put a collar on it with your address and telephone number on a disc or in a cylinder, like the one in this picture. Collars must have an elastic section so that the cat can escape if it gets the collar hooked on a tree. *Right:* Toys can be simple. Kittens will find endless ways to play with them – chewing them, pouncing on them or chasing them.

by. Open drawers and cupboards are irresistible too, so if you do not want the kitten rummaging about, make sure that everything is closed when it's around. The kitten could be trapped in a cupboard if someone closes the door without realizing that it has gone in to investigate.

A newspaper house is a good improvised toy. Just stand a partly opened newspaper on its side so that it makes a tunnel, and scrunch one end. The kitten will dive through the other end and spend quite a time trying to work out where the noise came from.

Cats are very fond of the smell of a plant called catnip, or catmint. Many of the toys sold in pet shops are filled with dried catnip and this encourages the cat to play with them. Catnip is also put on some scratching panels to help make the cat use it, but the effectiveness of this is questionable.

You can make a toy mouse with a piece of strong material that will not disintegrate when chewed. Sew it in a triangular mouse shape and fill it with dried catnip (you can buy this from the pet shop). Add a tail made of string,

A ball of string or wool is always a favourite for getting tangled up in. It's trying to find the end that causes all those problems.

sewn on firmly so that it cannot be chewed off and swallowed. Although this toy is static, the kitten will look on it as a potential opponent to roll around with. You can help by pulling the mouse around on a piece of string. This sort of play sharpens up the kitten's reflexes in preparation for hunting later on.

A ball – such as a table tennis ball which makes a noise when it rolls on an uncarpeted floor – is another favourite. So is a cotton reel. Toys can be suspended on a string so that they hang about an inch from the floor and swing as the kitten jumps at them. But make sure that the kitten cannot become caught up in the string.

Other improvised toys are balls of wool or string which can be unrolled and tangled around the furniture. Light feathers can be blown about as kittens love to chase them.

You might find that your kitten adopts something of the family's as a toy. For

Left: A child's soft toy can prove to be a close companion, even though you may not want the kitten to have it. But an opponent that doesn't fight back is good for the ego, and kittens play for hours with static toys like this, in some imaginary game. *Below left:* Things to climb into are interesting, too. A ball of string is a tight squeeze, but empty cardboard boxes make quite big caves for small kittens. They also like crawling under bedspreads, curtains and rugs, which is good practice for stalking through long grass later on.

example, a child's soft toy may prove to be just the right-sized opponent for a rough and tumble and, short of hiding the toy away, it will be hard to persuade the kitten to give up this idea. One favourite plaything may be selected to accompany the kitten into adulthood. It may carry the toy around in its mouth and have it nearby when it is going to sleep.

If no one in the family has time to play much with the kitten, it may become bored and lazy. In this case, it is better to get two kittens so that they can play together.

Working out a diet
The kitten uses up lots of energy at this age, and so seems to have a large appetite for its size. It grows quickly, too. At three months old, you can cut the number of meals to four if you have been giving five before. A little more variety can be introduced into the diet now. Cooked fish, for example, could make up one meal, and some cats like vegetables mixed in with a meat meal. A raw egg beaten up in milk is a nutritious snack. If the kitten shows any sign of diarrhoea, it may not be able to digest milk (see page 63). Try giving it diluted evaporated milk. If this fails milk should be cut out of the diet. Or you may find that some tinned foods do not agree with your cat, and these too should be eliminated.

At four months you can feed the kitten three times a day, though you may prefer to continue with four meals for a little longer. At this age the kitten should be eating about 6 oz (170 g) of food a day and can start having liver and other offal, or canned foods that include liver. It should still have two meat meals, and one or two milk meals, if it likes milk. Some cats like strange foods like cheese, and only trial and error will point out your cat's particular preferences.

Never give the cat chicken with bones in it as these splinter and may choke the cat. Keep its mealtimes regular, too, and do not feed it scraps from the table.

Though cats are known to be scavengers, they can be trained to take no interest in human mealtimes if they are never given food then. Apart from this, feeding between meals will produce a fat cat.

Between five and seven months, the number of meals can again be reduced to two or three. The amount of food should be increased gradually until at seven months the kitten is eating about 7 oz (200 g) a day.

Dried cat food can be introduced, and is very popular with most cats. It must be

Top: Longhaired cats need careful daily grooming to keep their coats in good condition. This should be started when they are kittens so that they get used to it. They have to be brushed and combed to keep the coat sleek and free from tangles. *Above:* Some cats can be trained to walk on a lead, though others refuse. Cats whose owners live in busy built-up areas can be exercised on a lead. As well as protecting it from traffic, this also ensures that the cat will not be chased or frightened by other animals.

moistened first until the kitten is used to it. Dried food in milk, water, or a gravy, could form the third meal. After a while, the kitten can be given the food dry, provided there is always a bowl of water nearby. But you must make sure that your cat drinks plenty of water. If it does not do so, cut dried food out of the diet – otherwise the cat may develop bladder trouble. If the cat drinks water, a little dried food makes a crunchy and nutritious snack which is good for its teeth.

At seven months the kitten has shed its milk teeth and begins to take on the appearance of an adult cat. It should be fed twice a day and its diet can be completely adult from now on. You may want to cut down the number of meals to one at about nine or ten months, but many cats prefer to have two meals a day.

Unless you vary the diet, the kitten may become faddy about its food and so not get properly balanced meals. Try a variety of things until you discover which ones it will eat, and do not let it get too set in its ways.

The amount a cat should eat as an adult depends on how big and how active it is. Estimate roughly $\frac{3}{4}$ oz (21 g) of food for each pound the cat weighs, and vary it up or down depending on the cat's shape; do not let it get too fat.

If the kitten is to stay indoors permanently (which some cats do quite happily, provided they are used to it from kittenhood), pots of grass should be left around for it to chew at. Cats chew grass for roughage and an indoor cat should not be deprived of the opportunity to do this. Otherwise, it may choose a substitute to chew, such as a houseplant or cut flowers.

It is good for kittens to get fresh air if this is possible. If you have a garden, you can let the kitten out as soon as it has been vaccinated. You will have to stay with it at first, particularly if you are near a road that it may roam towards.

Male kittens are more inclined to roam than females, and this habit may not be curbed until they are neutered at about five months old. So if your kitten tends to bolt away when allowed out, it should be kept under strict supervision until it has learned some road sense.

The greatest hazard to the small kitten is traffic. Even grown cats are not always very sensible about it. Kittens do learn that cars should be avoided when they are moving, but cats do not seem to be able to judge traffic speed accurately and may dash across a road in the path of an approaching car. Many cats are killed by traffic, particularly those which habitually roam out of their own back yard.

Above: Try to prevent a small kitten from going into the kitchen if you can. The kitchen is full of dangers and the kitten is bound to find them. *Right:* Electric cables are dangerous, too. They look interesting to play with, and a kitten's sharp teeth can pierce the outer casing and get to the live wires.

Collars, name tags and bells

If your cat is going to spend a fair amount of time out of doors, you may want it to wear a collar and name disc. You can have a disc inscribed with your address and telephone number so that if the cat does roam, at least there is a good chance of the neighbours getting to know it and returning it to you.

A cat collar should always have an elasticated section in it so that the cat can wriggle out if it gets caught when climbing a tree. Various types of collar, and name discs or cylinders, are available from pet shops.

If you want your cat to wear a collar, you should start getting it used to the idea when it is a kitten. In some cases, a collar will cause irritation and rub the fur off the neck. If this happens, take the collar off at once.

Put the collar on when the kitten is three or four months old. Take it off for grooming, and check each day that it is

Right: This kitten has climbed on to the wheel of a car, probably because the tyre is warm after a journey. In this case, the kitten is visible, but sometimes they are completely hidden when lying on the top of a wheel. Train your kitten as quickly as possible not to court disaster in this way.

not harming the kitten's coat. The collar should not be too tight.

Some collars have a bell on them, so that the cat can always be heard as it moves about. This is supposed to alert birds when the cat is stalking them, but the noise is more likely to drive the owner mad than save the lives of many birds. It does not take a cat long to work out what is hindering its hunting success, and it either learns to stalk without the bell ringing, or it manages to get rid of the bell altogether. One advantage of a bell is that it does help the owner to locate a kitten that refuses to come when it's called!

Keeping the kitten out of danger

In and out of doors, for the first few months the kitten is learning what is safe and what to avoid. You should try to keep it out of danger during this time. People may argue that stray and feral kittens manage to survive without an

Left: It may be easier to get up there than it is to get down again. You may have to rescue your kitten a few times when it is learning to climb – even adult cats get stuck sometimes. *Below:* A kitten that falls into a pot of paint, like this one is about to do, will be in a dreadful mess. The lead in paint is poisonous, and the kitten will try to lick it off clogged fur. Poison can be absorbed into the cat's system through the pads, so keep paints and disinfectants out of reach.

of being a nuisance about food if it sees it being prepared too much. If it knows there is no chance of titbits during cooking, it will soon lose interest in the kitchen when the family meals are being prepared.

Cats and kittens should never be allowed to walk across floors that have just been washed with disinfectant, which is absorbed into the pads and poisons the cat.

owner fussing over them, but many of the dangers to a small kitten come from being in a house with people. There are many things in the average household that can prove fatal to a prying kitten.

Electrical connections are dangerous because kittens will pounce at and play with anything that looks as if it will move. An electric cable looks ideal for a game. It wriggles as the kitten pounces, the kitten rolls over with it, clawing and biting with pin-sharp teeth. If it bites through the casing to the wires, it may be electrocuted.

So cables and kittens should be kept apart if possible. Cables should be tucked away under carpets, and the kitten should be spoken to sharply each time it tries this game. Say 'No' firmly and remove the kitten from the wire. If it sneaks back, do the same again until it gets bored and moves on to some other form of entertainment. Firm training will eventually stop this behaviour.

Getting trapped in open cupboards and drawers has already been mentioned. But there are other traps for a kitten, and these are not so easy to guard against. A boiler with an open back is an example; the back of a cooker or refrigerator is another. In fact, the kitchen is full of potential hazards, so try to keep the kitten out as much as you can. It is dangerous to have a kitten around when cooking is going on. It may follow closely on the cook's heels, and it is easy to turn and step on it, or trip over it. The kitten may be attracted by steam coming up from saucepans and jump up on the hot stove to investigate, or pull the pan off altogether. It may also get into the habit

Out of doors, the main dangers – apart from traffic – are that the kitten will get lost or stuck in a tree. If you do not let it go too far until it has got its bearings, it will probably not get lost. But very young kittens can get lost in long grass while out exploring. They stop and wail for help until they are rescued. Once a kitten has left its mother, though, it quickly begins to get a sense of direction and to learn where it lives.

Kittens also like to lie under or just behind parked cars, or sometimes on a wheel out of sight, so watch out for these dangers too.

Training the kitten

Cats can be trained to be obedient and well-behaved, though they are not so easy to train as dogs because they are more independent. Dogs depend on and are faithful to their owners, whereas cats behave in a less obviously devoted way. It is sometimes said that they do not know people and only care about where their next meal is coming from. This is not true. They get to know their owner, or family, and can be trained to recognize their name and to come when called. It is important to start teaching the kitten its name straightaway so that it can be called back when it goes outside.

You can teach the kitten its name by repeating it every time you are with it or training it. It will gradually learn to recognize the voice and then its own name.

Whenever the kitten does something it should not, such as scratching the furniture or jumping up at food, say 'No' in a firm voice. At the same time, remove the kitten from the chair, table or whatever, so that it knows that every time it does that thing it will be stopped. Cats can be contrary and do the things they know are forbidden on purpose, to see if they can run away before you scold them. But as they grow up these lessons usually pay off, and cats should always be trained so that they are not a nuisance about the house.

Tricks are another matter, and most cats do not care to obey commands in the same way that a dog will. Cats have been taught tricks, but these are often things they want to do anyway, such as sitting up on their hind legs and clapping paws, or boxing with their front paws.

If your cat spends quite a bit of time out of doors, it may decide that it wants to go out at night as it gets older. Cats often like to hunt at night. However, unless you have a cat door (see below) or a method by which the cat can get in and out at night, this is not a very good idea. Cats should never be forced out against their will. Even if a cat wants to

go, it may change its mind when the rain pours down and the family is fast asleep. Then the cat gets a soaking if it cannot find somewhere to shelter, or someone gets woken up by persistent mewing outside a window.

The cat should get used to a bedtime routine. This means that it goes to its usual sleeping place, whether this is a proper basket or a place of its own choosing (so long as this is not on someone's bed). It should have a sanitary tray for the night, though it can be let out just before bedtime and called in again, The procedure will depend on your cat's habits, mealtimes and so on, but most cats appreciate the warmth of a dry bed on a cold winter's night.

Fitting a cat door

There is some advantage in fitting a cat door if you can. These can be made at

Sharp objects like this bamboo wood can damage the delicate inside of a kitten's mouth. Make sure that toys do not have sharp edges or bits that can be chewed off to make a dangerous edge. Try to persuade the kitten against biting sharp objects by removing them, or the kitten, when you see it happening.

home or bought from a pet shop, and they come in various styles. Basically, what is needed is a flap cut in an outside door and hinged so that it opens both ways. The advantage is that if everyone in the family is out for the day, the cat can come and go as it pleases. It can come in and go out at night or during the day without having to mew at the door each time. The disadvantage is that your cat's friends may decide to come in too, though cats are quite firm about guarding their own territory.

A cat door should be fitted when the cat is still a kitten so that it gets used to using it early. You could start at four months if your kitten is a stay-at-home type, or after it has been neutered at five months if it is a male that is inclined to roam.

Train the kitten to use the door at meal times to start with. The best way is to put its food on the wrong side of the door; that is, put the kitten on the outside and the food on the inside. Open the flap a bit so that the kitten smells its food and also notices that the flap is moveable. When it has used the flap once, it may remember for ever – or it may need one or two more lessons first. Change the order round, so that the kitten realizes that it has to go out through the flap as well. Always give it its meal as soon as it has come in through the door during training.

Some cat flaps can be locked in position. This is useful if you want to keep the cat in for a time – or if you want to keep it or other cats out.

Once the kitten is allowed out regularly, it can be taught to go outside rather than using its sanitary tray. Some cats take a while to understand this, and sometimes come in from the garden to use the tray. Other cats – ones which have been allowed out from the beginning – do not have to be told.

To train the kitten, move its tray from its regular position to a little nearer the door. When the kitten has got used to this, move the tray to just inside the door, then just outside. Finally, put the kitten in the garden when it is about to use its tray, perhaps with some litter on the earth to help it understand.

Kittens are company for one another, so if you do not have much time to play with your kitten, it may be best to get it a playmate. Then you will not need to worry that it is bored while you are out.

Though the cat may prefer to go outside once it has learned this, a tray should always be provided as well.

Neutering and spaying
Cats which are not going to be used for breeding kittens (see page 67) should be neutered in the case of males, or spayed in the case of females. Otherwise, tomcats will roam and make the house smell, and females will produce endless litters of kittens that you will have to find homes for – often a difficult task!

Neutering or spaying can be done from four months onwards, though the

Grooming a long-haired cat

Longhaired cats need careful daily grooming, otherwise their coats become tangled and matted. They may also swallow loose hairs when washing their coats. You will need a fairly stiff brush and a wide-toothed comb. Both these can be bought from pet shops. You will also need some talcum powder. Use special grooming powder or baby powder.

Rub the powder into the fur thoroughly, separating the hairs with your fingers. Leave for a while to absorb any grease.

Brush the powder out, making sure that loose hairs and dust are removed at the same time. Make sure that all the powder has been thoroughly removed.

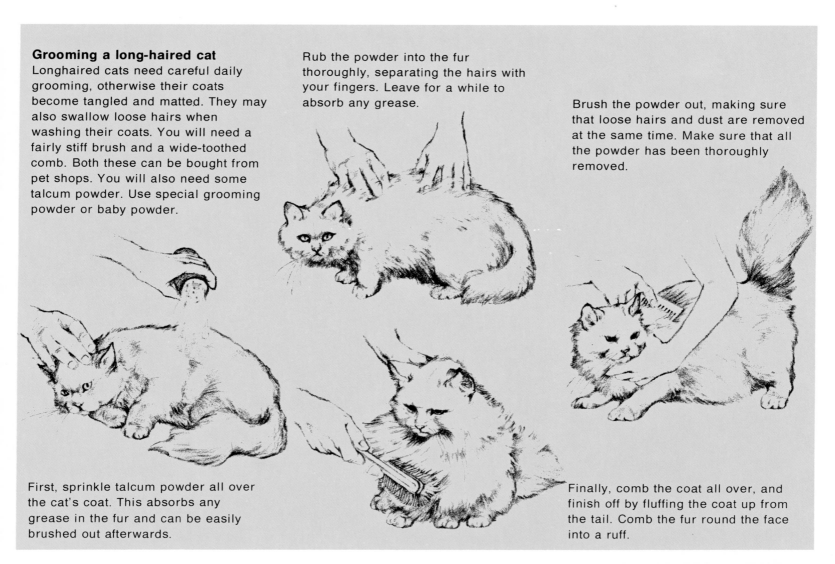

First, sprinkle talcum powder all over the cat's coat. This absorbs any grease in the fur and can be easily brushed out afterwards.

Finally, comb the coat all over, and finish off by fluffing the coat up from the tail. Comb the fur round the face into a ruff.

Right: A cat door gives a cat far more flexibility to come and go as it pleases. If you plan to fit one, do so when the cat is still a kitten.

standard time is at between five or six months. Adult cats can be operated on too, but it is best to get the job done when they are kittens.

Your local vet will give you information about the age the kitten should be, and the procedure at his particular surgery. The operation is less complicated for male cats and they can usually come home the same day or first thing the next morning, when they have come round from the anaesthetic. They will be their usual selves after about 24 hours.

Female cats need a slightly more complicated internal operation but they will be fine again after two days at the most.

Neutered males tend to lose interest in roaming off, preferring home and the fireside. Once out of kittenhood, they will grow bigger than tomcats and may put on too much weight if they do not take much exercise. Neutered or spayed cats generally make more friendly pets, though they still continue to hunt, fight with other cats and so on. They make just as efficient mousers, too.

Chapter five
Understanding your Cat

Cats are hunters and even the most docile and well fed pet shows another side of its nature when it catches sight of a mouse or bird. With body low, it tenses its muscles ready to pounce.

A miaow is not just a miaow to a cat. It is part of its own language, by which it expresses itself to other cats, and to people. The sound language of the cat consists of miaowing, purring, hissing, howling, growling, and chirruping. Cats also have a complicated body language – the tail, ears, mouth, paws, and position of the body all show anger, fear, watchfulness, contentment, and other emotions.

The language and behaviour of the cat is very interesting. The cat is a solitary hunter, stalking its prey by night. It can climb, balance, run, jump, pounce, and leap. The same animal, at other times, can be a soft, sleepy pet, rolling and stretching, playing and kneading with its front paws. So what does cat language and behaviour mean?

Understanding sounds and movements

One expert on cats has counted 100 or more different sounds, which include the various types of mew and chirrup. The cat combines these with movements of the tail, ears, paws and body to make very definite points. For example, a growl of anger will be accompanied by flattening of the ears. The coat stands on end to make the body look bigger, and the pose is defensive – prepared to attack if necessary, yet tending to back off.

An arched back combined with fur standing on end and a hissing growl means fear. The tail is fluffed out – another sign of fear. If the tail is waving gently, the cat is happy and enjoying the situation. But if the tail is whipping back and forth like a lash, the cat is annoyed and brewing up to a fight or attack.

Cats sometimes trot along with tail held erect, especially if they are walking

Hunting is a natural instinct to a cat. Even a well-fed pet cat hunts for fun, though if it is too fat and lazy it will not be very efficient. As well as rodents, cats kill birds and insects.

along with their owner, or going to greet a friend, or think it is a meal time. The tail held erect with a slight crook at the top means that the cat is in a good mood.

Purring normally means pleasure – for example, a cat sitting on a person's lap being stroked will often purr. It can occasionally mean that the cat is in pain, but generally speaking it is a sign of contentment.

Your cat may greet you with a chirruping sound – for example, if you call its name, or have just returned home and the cat is pleased to see you. This is its way of saying 'hello'. The miaow that means 'Open this door' or 'I want to come in', on the other hand, is a much more insistent and piercing sound. The miaow of displeasure – when the cat is shut in somewhere against its will, perhaps – is also very distinctive. It is loud and persistent and leaves the owner in no doubt that the cat is displeased. However, a miaow that rises in tone – 'Miaow' – seems to be another way of greeting owner or friend.

The ears

Ears flattened means anger or fear, and if they are beginning to go back, the cat is warning you, or another cat, that it is getting fed up with the way things are going. A cat listens to all that is going on around it, and its ears flick back and forth to pick up sounds.

When the cat is alert and watchful, its ears will be pricked and forward. Round eyes and upright ears mean curiosity and interest in something that is going on nearby.

The whiskers

The cat's whiskers are long and very sensitive. They are an essential part of its hunting equipment, because they warn the cat of obstacles which it cannot see. It is said that a cat will not go through a space which is narrower than the full span of face and whiskers, but this is not

An arched back with the fur fluffed up is a sign of fear and aggression. The cat fluffs up its fur and tail to try to make itself look bigger and more ferocious to its opponents.

the real function of the whiskers.

The whiskers can detect changes in the environment, such as changes in the air pressure when there is an obstacle in the way. They then send messages back to the cat's brain via its lips. So even when it cannot see properly – and, whatever people may say, cats cannot see in complete darkness – its whiskers help it to discover where it is and how to find its way around.

The cat's eyebrows, ear tufts and the hair on its wrists are also very sensitive and are used in much the same way as the whiskers.

The claws and paws

The other vital weapon for hunting is the set of claws. Cats' claws can be in or out. When cats are playing, they use soft paws with no sign of the claws. But when they are catching prey or climbing, the claws come out to make sharp and lethal tools for the work in hand. Some people have their cats' claws removed so that they cannot scratch the furniture, but this means that the cat can no longer climb, and so one of its methods of self-protection is lost. The practice of declawing is frowned on by many people, and declawed cats cannot be entered for shows. Many vets refuse to declaw cats.

When a cat is happy, it often kneads at a soft object. For example, if your cat is sitting on your knee, it may start to knead at your legs. Or it may knead a toy or ball of wool. It pushes its paws back and forth, like someone kneading dough, and the claws go in and out at the same time. This can be a rather painful process if the cat chooses you to knead at. The habit is one carried on from kittenhood. Little kittens knead the mother cat when they are suckling, and kneading and purring in

Left: The cat uses its tail to show its mood. This cat is happy and contented with life, as is shown by the upward pointing tail with a crook at the end. A lashing tail means anger, though a gently waving one is another sign of a happy cat. *Below:* Ears are another tell-tale sign of mood. These two cats are about to fight, and the one on the right of the picture is the attacker. The other cat's ears are flattened, showing that it is afraid and is retreating, though it is prepared to put up a fight if necessary. The cats are growling and spitting at one another, another sure sign of anger. It is easy to understand a cat's moods once you recognize the signals they give.

a kitten or cat is a sign of relaxed contentment.

The paws are very sensitive and are used for investigation – patting and sniffing at things help to solve the mystery of what they are.

The cat as a hunter

It is fascinating to watch a cat stalking its prey. Its movements are lithe and silent, and it instinctively chooses whatever cover is available until it is ready for the final pounce.

Kittens instinctively learn to hunt, though until they are three months old they only play at it. When they are only a

few weeks old, they start to pretend by hunting the other kittens in the litter in mock pouncing and biting games. They will also lie in wait to pounce at people, particularly if they have no other animal to play with. To start with, a small kitten takes a long time to get round to pouncing. It crouches low, shuffling its back legs in readiness. Its eyes are wide and its expression alert. Then it may pounce just a few inches at an imaginary enemy. But it is all good practice.

Some people are surprised when an innocent kitten catches its first creature. Hunting does not seem to go with kittenhood. Yet hunting is so instinctive to the cat that even a well-fed pet cat will hunt just for the sport. It may not eat its prey at all, but lack of necessity will not stop it from stalking anything that moves. Kittens and cats will chase insects for hours, too, jumping and slapping against windows and walls to catch a fly. They eat the insects they catch. Grasshoppers are a favourite to catch as they jump through the grass. Be careful that your cat does not chase wasps or bees, particularly in late summer when they are getting drowsy. The cat may get stung on paw or mouth.

People who keep cats as mousers sometimes believe that they do their job

Above: This cat seems to be roaring with laughter, and cats often do look amused. The grin shows the cat's teeth, which are typical of meat-eaters. The four canines are long and sharp and are used for killing prey with a bite in the neck. The incisors are also sharp and can strip meat from bone very effectively. But the cat cannot chew. It eats by tearing, biting and swallowing pieces of meat. Its digestive processes break down chunks of meat.
Left: The tongue is rough because it is covered with tiny lumps called papillae, forming a sort of comb for cleaning fur.

better if they are not given much food. This is not so. In fact, a hunting cat is more efficient if it is properly fed and in good condition, even though feral and stray cats do survive in the wild by hunting.

Unfortunately, some cats do not know the difference between mice and rats, and the fat, friendly robin perched on the window sill. To the cat, all are fair game. Naturally, it is more difficult to catch a bird, which can take off into the air, but birds do get caught and this can be upsetting for the owner. Cats sometimes lay their kill on the doorstep as a present for their owners. But nothing will make

How a cat falls

Cats can afford to be fearless climbers because they do not get dizzy and, when they do fall, they can turn their bodies in mid-air so that they usually land on their feet. This ability is called the self-correcting reflex. If the cat is upside-down at the start of a fall, it can turn its body through 180° and position its legs to take the impact – provided, of course, that the fall is not too short to allow this full turn. So cats do not often break bones through falling, even from quite a height.

your cat understand that you do not appreciate such gifts, and that birds should be left to fly free, so cat owners must be able to accept these facts.

Cats have very strong muscles in their hind legs, allowing them to collect themselves and pounce powerfully on their prey from some distance away. The prey is gripped in the front paws, claws fully extended, and the kill is made by a bite in the neck.

The well-fed pet cat may not eat its prey, or may eat just part of it. It often eats part of a bird, for example – if it can catch one, that is. But cats that are overfed become lazy and are not good hunters. A pet cat in prime condition makes a good hunter and mouser.

Catching birds is the most difficult of the cat's hunting activities. It requires a great deal of guile and stealth. The hunting position is a crouch, eyes wide and watchful, ears pricked to pick up any sounds that may help it to locate the exact position of its prey, without being seen. Sometimes the cat crouches and watches for a long time before attacking. The movements towards the prey, before getting into position for the kill, are low, long and silent. The cat's body and head are kept low, the ears flat and the face

Below: When a cat wakes up, it often stretches every bit of its body. The body sometimes looks twice the usual length, or is arched into a semi-circle by the strong back muscles.

forward. It is in this sort of movement that the grace of the cat can be seen. When it is close enough, it prepares to attack, and finally springs forward with great strength and accuracy.

The cat does not always kill its prey first time. It may taunt it with pats and swipes of the paw before killing it. And it may play with it after it is dead, too, tossing it back and forth until it gets bored with the game. This is all part of the sport of hunting.

Climbing and balancing

Another demonstration of the cat's lithe strength can be seen in its climbing activities. Little kittens climb up curtains for practice, and kittens and cats instinctively climb trees for fun and self-protection. They sometimes get stuck, but they can climb and balance their way out of most situations. The claws are extended, and these together with strong muscles along the back and in the legs make it possible for the cat to haul itself up a vertical surface. The tail is useful for balancing. The cat moves it to distribute its weight evenly. This enables it to run along narrow branches and fences like a tightrope walker.

Washing

Cats keep themselves as clean as they can (though they still need help from their owners to keep their coats in really good condition). After a meal, a cat sits down and washes its coat thoroughly. It

Above: Cats spend a good deal of their time asleep, and they seem to sleep peacefully in the most uncomfortable positions. They will lie upside-down, curled up, or stretched out, and move about, often without waking up. *Right:* Washing is instinctive and cats hate to be dirty. They wash their coats thoroughly after every meal, using their rough tongues to scrape away every trace of dirt.

has a rough tongue that can get into the fur, removing any bits of dirt. It washes its face with a licked paw, systematically covering every inch of head and ears, re-licking the paw as necessary. The only place it cannot reach is at the very back of its neck.

When it has carefully washed its face, using both forepaws, it turns its attention to the rest of the body. It twists its head round to lick shoulders and back, and gets into all sorts of contortions to reach hindquarters and tail.

The washing process takes some time. Any foreign bodies, such as burrs, are bitten out of the coat, and the paws are carefully cleaned between the toes and round the pads. The cat sits up on its

the time a kitten goes to its new home, it can wash itself quite competently. It spends a long time on this after its meals and may wash in between times too. Cats sometimes wash as soon as they wake up, or when they have been outside. They also wash when they are upset or embarrassed. This has nothing to do with keeping clean. It is the same sort of action as a person fidgeting or looking all round the room in embarrassment.

A bored cat may wash itself too much, and lick parts of its coat bare. But a kitten or cat that leads a lively and interesting life should have no problems of this kind.

Cats hate to be dirty and this is why their sanitary trays must be kept clean, and their coats brushed and combed regularly.

Sleeping

Cats sleep in a variety of poses and contortions which once again show the flexibility of their bodies. They often sleep curled up in a ball, with the tail wrapped round paws and nose. Sometimes they curl paws over nose, or stretch out to a great length. Some cats, and particularly kittens, sleep on their backs with their legs up in the air.

Cats have two sorts of sleep. One is a light doze – from which the term 'catnap' comes. In this, the cat sleeps for a short time and wakes quickly. Often, it seems to be asleep, yet its eyes are partly open and it appears to be able to hear what is going on around it.

When the cat is properly asleep, it seems to dream in the same way that people do. It twitches and turns in its sleep, sometimes making slight noises or

Above: This ferocious looking cat has its claws fully extended to attack. It is ready to drive its teeth into an enemy if necessary, and it is hard to imagine that such a creature could ever be curled up on the hearthrug. But the claws can quickly retract, and make soft paws for playing friendly games. *Right:* The cat is lithe and agile, and this picture demonstrates the grace of a cat on the move. It runs in a fluid movement with great coordination and speed. It makes no noise as it moves so prey is not warned of its approach. All these factors combine to make the cat the perfect hunting animal.

hind legs to wash the stomach fur, which is longer and may have tangles in it. These are also bitten out.

Mother cats lick their kittens from birth, and in this way the tiny kittens get the habit themselves and begin to try and wash at about three or four weeks old. By

Cats use their claws for climbing, too. Cats can haul themselves up vertical surfaces, such as tree tunks, by digging their claws into the bark and pulling themselves up using the strong muscles in the back and legs. Declawing a cat deprives it of the ability to climb, which is one of its forms of self-protection.

purring. What a cat dreams about, no one knows, but it certainly needs plenty of deep sleep to keep fit and well. It sleeps for several hours at a stretch. For example, a cat that likes to go out hunting at night will probably sleep for most of the day. Or if it has plenty of exercise during the day, it will sleep solidly through the night. But it will still take catnaps during its waking hours.

Cats like to sleep in the sunshine and lie for hours on a sunny window ledge or doorstep. If it gets too hot, they sometimes creep into the middle of a flower bed, among the plants and shrubs, for a bit of shade.

Territorial rights

A cat normally chooses the same few places to sleep, which may or may not include a special cat basket. This instinct is all part of the cat's strong feeling for territorial rights. Indoors, this instinct shows itself in the way a cat will often have its own favourite places to sleep or sit. Persuading it that its chosen favourite territory is forbidden can be difficult.

Out of doors, a cat jealously guards its own territory from other cats. Its territory may be the garden or yard, or just a small area outside the door. It may crouch on the doorstep in a threatening pose, daring the next-door cat to come any nearer. It will probably chase away or fight with any cats that come in, too. Cats do wander from one garden to another, so they do not have the same feeling about keeping off other cats' territories as they do for protecting their own.

A tomcat which has not been neutered has an unpleasant habit of spraying the boundaries of its territory so that it carries his smell. Unfortunately, he does this indoors as well as outside. This is the chief reason for neutering male cats that are not required for breeding as soon as they are old enough. Neutered males, and females, spayed or not, do not spray their territory. Tomcats are also more inclined to fight over territorial rights, and many wandering toms become battle-scarred, with scratched faces and torn ears.

Cats also mark their territory with scent glands on the head and body. When they rub their heads or faces along a chair or other piece of furniture, they are

Above: The climbing frame effect of this trellis allows the cat to move in all directions, up, down or sideways. The paws and claws are used for gripping, though the technique is rather different from climbing a tree, and this cat looks a bit apprehensive about the whole venture. *Left:* Round, watchful eyes and ears pricked mean that the cat is watchful and concentrating all its attention on the matter in hand – in this case, stalking prey. The cat stalks by moving silently and stealthily, with body close to the ground and eyes fixed on the prey. It may watch the prey for a long time, waiting for the right moment to make the final pounce.

establishing their territorial rights over it. A cat also establishes its relationship with its owner by rubbing against the owner's legs. This is a sign of greeting and pleasure, but the glands on the forehead and mouth also leave the cat's scent on the owner. This is not noticeable to humans. But cats can smell each other's territories, or places where another cat has been.

Sense of smell

Cats have a very strong sense of smell, and they do not only use this to detect one another's territories. They have very definite likes and dislikes about the smells around the house. For example, some cats do not like the smell of cigarette smoke, and will leave the room if someone starts smoking. They do not as a rule like the smell of alcohol or citrus fruits. But they love the smell of catmint and have been known to roll ecstatically in a bed where it is growing.

Running and jumping

But all this purring contentment does not prevent even the most fluffy and docile pet cat from putting on a great turn of speed and agility when it wants to, and not just on hunting expeditions. Cats can jump from great heights, landing on their soft pads. Their strength in jumping comes from their hindquarter muscles. These allow the cat to control its movements perfectly, with the muscles taking the strain of the body as it prepares to leap. Arching of the back is made possible by strong back muscles, which can turn the cat's body into a semi-circle when it is angry or having a good stretch after a sleep.

Fighting

Fighting normally takes place between two tomcats, perhaps because there is a female nearby. Tomcats fight over their territories, too, and even if your cat is neutered, a tom may still attack it. Sometimes the attack comes to nothing, and one of the cats gives in and slinks away. But if they do decide to fight (and it will normally be two toms who go through with it), each cat tries to make itself look bigger and more formidable by fluffing out coat and tail. They gather their strength in hunched shoulders, ready to pounce. Then they growl at one another. With their backs arched, fur erect, ears back, lips drawn back in a snarl, it is hard to imagine that these cats could be pets. But a serious attack means that the cats go for each other, biting and scratching, clawing lumps of fur out of each other's coats, and rolling over and over in combat. This sort of behaviour in tomcats is the reason that those allowed to roam free, mating and fighting, often lose their looks and become battle-scarred with bad coats and wounds on their faces.

The cats' eyes

The night prowler, whether hunting, fighting or just enjoying the night air, needs one other important asset; the ability to see in the dark. Cats cannot see in total blackness, but they can see very much more than most animals can in near-darkness. This is because the pupils of the cat's eyes can open very wide to let in the maximum amount of light. There is also a reflector at the back of the eye which allows the maximum amount

of light to be absorbed. In very bright light, the pupils become very thin slits so that the cat is not dazzled.

So if you see a cat in a dark room or in twilight, you will notice that its eyes shine and the pupils are large and black. The shininess comes from the reflector at the back of the eye, and the pupil is large to let in all the light there is. If you suddenly turn on a light or shine a torch

Top: Cats can run along very narrow surfaces, such as fences and tree branches. They use the tail to help them balance. *Above:* Cats often taunt their prey before killing it – surely one of their less endearing habits, but one that is typical of all members of the family *felidae* from the mighty lions of the African Savannah to the tiniest domestic kitten at your fireside.

at the cat, the pupils quickly narrow into slits to compensate for the change.

Cats also have 'binocular vision', like all meat-eating animals. The eyes are set in the front of the head so that they can see their prey. The eyes of an animal that does not have to hunt, such as a horse or a cow, are set to the sides of the face, so they can spot attackers creeping up behind them.

Cats have a very wide area of vision. The area of one eye's vision overlaps with the area of the other eye's. So the cat can see everything in front of it with no blind spots, and can focus very accurately on prey that is some distance away. It can also judge how far away the prey is. This accuracy when hunting or playing makes it surprising that the cat seems to have difficulty judging the speed of approaching traffic, which seems to be the reason why so many cats get run over.

It has often been said that cats are colour blind, but it is now thought that they can see some colour. Though they cannot see colours as vividly as human beings can, they do seem to be able to tell the difference between colours.

Can your cat understand you?

So it is possible to understand what a cat is doing or trying to say. It has a definite language of its own. But is there any point in trying to understand your cat? Are you going to get anything in return? Has a cat got the brain to try and understand its owner?

The answer to these questions is 'yes'. Though traditionally the dog is man's best friend and the cat is the comfort-loving loner, cats are very intelligent animals. They often use this intelligence in ways which suit them best, it is true, but they do get to know quite a lot about their owners and learn to fit into the household.

The cat's hearing is very acute and it soon learns to recognize the sounds which affect its own lifestyle – the sound of the refrigerator door, or a tin being opened, or the sound of its food-cupboard door. Familiar sounds like these bring the cat running hopefully into the kitchen.

It hears other things too. It learns to recognize the doorbell and the telephone, and soon knows which is which, running in the right direction to be in on whatever is happening. It knows the sound of the family car approaching and runs to the window or door, or to greet its owner if it is outside. It also seems to be able to recognize its owner's footsteps and is often in position behind the door even before the key has been put in the lock.

The cat's instinct about things is

probably why it has always had connections with myth and magic. It is said to have a sixth sense which tells it when some disaster is going to happen. There are stories of cats trying to warn their owners about things, or taking protective action themselves.

One instinct cats certainly have is the ability to find their way back to an old home, often travelling miles to get there.

There are reports in the United States of cats travelling from California to Oklahoma, from New York to California, and from Louisiana to Texas, in each case taking several months to make the journey and having to cross miles and

White cats usually have blue or orange eyes. Sometimes they have one blue eye and one orange or copper-coloured eye. These are called Odd-eyed Whites.

miles of unfamiliar terrain. Sometimes they even swim rivers during their journey, though cats do not really like water and only swim if they have to. (An exception is the Turkish cat, which swims for pleasure.)

There are many stories of cats trying to comfort owners in distress. They will often jump up on the owner's lap, patting or licking away tears with a look of concern on their faces.

Some cats learn to open doors by themselves, though they have not always got the strength to do it properly. But they notice that their owner opens a door by turning a knob, so they stand up on their hind legs and try to turn the knob with both front paws. They can open doors with handles, again standing up on hind legs and pushing the handle down. Most cats open doors that are ajar by curling a paw round the edge and pulling the door open.

They also have a knack of knowing which room someone is in, if they are outside and want to be let in through the relevant window, And this is in daylight, with no lights to give clues.

So a cat makes an intelligent companion with a character and personality all of its own, and it is interesting to try to understand how your cat thinks.

Cats can see in the dark because the pupils of their eyes can open very wide to let in any light there is. In the top picture, the eyes are watchful, with the pupils open quite wide. In the lower picture, the cat is looking into a bright light, because the pupils have closed up into slits. The eyes close up like this so that the cat is not dazzled.

Chapter six
Going on Holiday

When you go away on holiday, plan in advance. Find a reliable neighbour to look after your pet, or put it in a cattery. Whatever you do, don't leave it to fend for itself.

One of the problems of owning a pet is that you have to make arrangements for it if you go away from home, even for a day or two. This is something that many people forget in the first enthusiasm of getting a cat or a dog of their own. The animal cannot just be left to fend for itself.

Catteries

If you are going away for a holiday of a week or two, it is probably best to leave your cat in a boarding cattery. These places are specially designed to look after cats while their owners are away. Your vet or an animal welfare society may be able to recommend a good cattery in your area, or you can look them up in a trade telephone directory, or ask friends or neighbours who have cats if they can recommend one.

Some catteries are indoor ones, and others are partly indoor and partly outdoor. In each type, the cat has an individual pen with sleeping quarters and an exercise area. The best catteries for the cat's health are the type that have a warm sleeping house, with enough room for the cat's bed, feeding bowls and sanitary tray, and an outside run where it can exercise in the fresh air. The sleeping house should really be big enough for the cat to be able to exercise in too, so that it can stretch its legs when it is raining or cold.

The only problem with indoor catteries is that, if the pens are too close together, the cats may pick up infections from each other. Indoor catteries should have plenty

Left: It is wrong to think that your cat will not be able to cope if you go on holiday. Do not be put off by a plaintive expression – cats can adapt very well provided they are well looked after in their owners' absence. *Right:* A cattery with outdoor runs is the best type as the cats can exercise and climb in the fresh air. But remember to book up well in advance, not at the last minute.

of room and good ventilation.

It is a good idea to try and find out as much as you can about a cattery before booking your cat into it. You may be able to find out about the ones in your area from neighbours or friends who have cats, or someone in the family may be able to go along and have a look at the cattery.

Good catteries get booked up months ahead, so it's best not to leave it until the last minute to book in your cat.

A fortnight in a cattery may sound a lonely existence for your pet, but good cattery owners give their charges plenty of attention and affection, and make sure that they are well fed and comfortable. Most catteries will also ask for a vet's certificate to show that the cat is in the best of health and that it has been vaccinated against Feline Infectious Enteritis. This precaution lessens the chances of any infection spreading among the cats – always a problem when a number of cats are kept together.

Cats can be taught to travel, and can sometimes be taken on holiday. But they do like their own familiar surroundings, so may try and rush off when they find themselves in a strange place.

Leaving the cat with a neighbour

There are some alternatives to the boarding cattery. You may be able to leave your cat with a neighbour, or someone may be prepared to come in once or twice a day to feed your pet and clean out the sanitary tray, or let the cat out for a spell in the fresh air. But you must be sure that the neighbour is reliable and that the cat will be properly looked after while you are away. Cats like to stay in familiar surroundings though, and if you do have someone who will look after the cat in its own home, this can be quite a good solution.

Taking your cat with you

You can, of course, take your cat with you on holiday, though you must

This cat looks quite relaxed in its holiday cattery. Try and find out as much as you can about a cattery before booking your cat in, and if possible look at the cats that are already there to see if they seem fit and content.

remember that if you live in Britain and are going abroad for a holiday, you will not be able to bring the cat back into the country without putting it into quarantine for six months. Different countries have different quarantine regulations, and cats sometimes have to have certain injections before being allowed into another country. So you should check on all this very carefully.

But if you are not going abroad, you may be able to take your cat without too much trouble, though not all cats like to travel. If you are going to a hotel, you will have to check that cats are allowed there.

If you are taking the cat on a journey, the first essential is a good travelling carrier. There are plenty to choose from in pet shops. It should be strong enough to keep the cat in, even if it is frightened, and should also be comfortable inside, as the cat may have to be in there for some considerable length of time so should be able to stretch its legs.

Training a cat to travel

A cat should really be trained from kittenhood to be put in a carrier and to travel in a car. A grown cat may be frightened if it is suddenly shut away like this. Of course, it is not always possible to predict whether your cat is going to travel or not, but you will have to take it to the vet every now and then, and maybe to cat shows, so it is wise to try and get it used to travelling.

You can leave the carrier, with the door open, for the kitten to investigate as part of its playtime. It can sniff around and dive in and out, so that the carrier soon becomes familiar. You can try to persuade the kitten to sleep in the carrier sometimes. Put in a blanket, made into a warm nest, and when the kitten seems sleepy, put it into the carrier. The important thing is that the kitten feels safe and secure in the carrier, and not that it is a prison cell.

If the kitten does not take to the carrier, try feeding it a meal in there. Leave the door open whenever the kitten is in the carrier at this stage, so that it does not panic.

The next stage is to shut the door of the carrier for short spells. Make sure that the kitten has a comfortable place to lie

down, and put a familiar toy or two and some food in with it. Let the kitten out and make a fuss of it. Keep the times in the carrier short at first so that the kitten learns to like going in.

Once the kitten is used to the carrier, you can start taking it on short journeys in a car, if this is how you are going to travel most. Cats may be frightened by the motion of a car and may wail at first. But they get used to it if trained early enough.

Never be tempted to have a cat loose in the car. It may lie on the back seat at first, but it may panic at some stage and start rushing around. This is distracting for the driver, and can also be dangerous if the cat gets in the way of the brake pedal. It may also jump out and run away if there is an accident, or when you stop for a meal or at a garage. So, unless there is someone who can keep a firm hold on the cat, it should be kept in its carrier during the journey, and should always be put into it before the car doors are opened.

Cats must be in carriers to travel on buses, trains and aeroplanes. Usually the cat in its carrier can travel with its owner, but sometimes it has to go in the luggage compartment. You must check first what

Choosing a travelling basket
There are many types of carrier to choose from. Some of them are big enough for more than one cat at a time; some are made of wicker and look like hampers; others are made of perspex, so that the cat can see out. Whichever sort you decide on, there are one or two points to bear in mind. The carrier must be high enough for the cat to stand up in it, and must be big enough for the cat to be able to move around on a long journey. There should be adequate ventilation, and the catch must be firm, so that the cat cannot work it loose and escape.

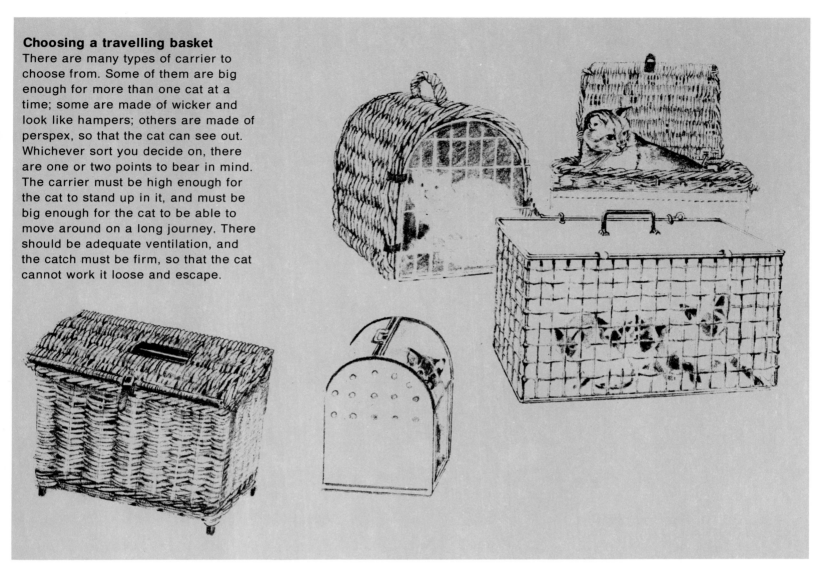

A neighbour may offer to take your cat into his or her own home, but this will be strange for the cat unless it knows the neighbour's house already. It may be best if the neighbour feeds the cat in your house, and lets it out each day.

the regulations are. This applies particularly to travel by air, as different airlines have different rules.

Unfortunately, cats are less reliable than dogs when it comes to keeping track of them. The main problem about taking your cat on holiday may not be the journey, but what happens when you get there. Cats like familiar surroundings and may become confused if suddenly expected to spend two weeks in a strange place. You will have to keep an eye on the cat when it goes out, to make sure that it does not run away and get lost.

There are many stray cats in most countries of the world. A lot of strays have become so because owners found that after a while they could no longer be bothered to look after their pets. Holiday time is the worst of all for this attitude because it does take forward planning to decide what to do with your pet. But there is always some answer, and it is cruel to turn a cat out to look after itself.

Chapter seven
Keeping a Cat Healthy

Cats are normally healthy creatures and hardly ever
need to see a vet. Good food, regular exercise,
careful grooming and, of course, plenty of affection
should keep your pet in the peak of condition.

Keeping a cat healthy does not mean
fussing over it all the time, but seeing
that it has a good mixed diet, is
groomed daily, has sufficient exercise and
is shown plenty of affection. The majority
of cats live long lives – twenty years or
more sometimes – and most never need
a vet's attention.

A cat that is not well soon shows it,
and goes downhill rapidly. It is always
wise to get to know your nearest vet and
to have his telephone number to hand in
case of emergency.

If a cat is off its food, sits with head
down, and appears to have little interest
in anything, it is best to call the vet or to
take it there, rather than ring around to
friends for advice or try treating it
yourself.

Serious illnesses

There are two serious illnesses that
may be contracted by kittens and cats.
The first is Feline Infectious Enteritis (FIE),
a disease that particularly affects kittens
and old cats, if they have not been
vaccinated. The symptoms are a rise in
temperature at first, then a slight fall. A
cat's normal temperature is 100.5–101°F
(38–38.3°C). The cat refuses to eat, and
sits with its head over its water bowl, but
not drinking. There may be slight
vomitting, with the animal crying when
touched or picked up. Death may occur
within hours. It is therefore most
important to have the kitten vaccinated at
the age recommended by the vet, as it
does give very effective protection.

This illness can be passed to other cats
through clothing, newspapers, feeding
bowls, or anything that has been touched
by the cat or even the owner. Should a
cat or kitten die of FIE, thorough
disinfection of the house and contents
will probably be necessary. No new kitten
should be introduced for some months.

This black cat is obviously very healthy.
His condition is excellent and his eyes
are bright.

The other serious illness is the one
usually known as cat flu, which has
several other long names. It is caused by
one virus or more. Vaccines for this are
effective in some cases, but not all. Here
again, the vet's advice should be sought
as to whether a kitten should be
vaccinated or not.

The symptoms are similar to that of a
cold, with running eyes and nose,
coughing and sneezing. If neglected, cat
flu can be fatal to young kittens and can
leave cats with snuffles. Weeks of nursing
and very careful attention may be
necessary before the animal will once
again be in tip-top condition. It is highly
contagious and can be passed on to
other kittens and cats.

There is another elusive yet fatal
disease that can affect cats. This is a form
of leukaemia (FeLV). There are varying
symptoms which can only be confirmed
by a vet. It is usually found where a
number of cats are kept in close
proximity. It is advisable for anyone
deciding to buy an expensive pedigree
kitten to ask if the breeder's stock has
been FeLV tested.

Looking after a sick cat

Good home nursing plays a most
important part during or after any illness
if the cat is to make a complete recovery.
Cats, particularly Siamese, seem to give
up so easily. They will need constant
attention. Make a warm bed, such as a
cardboard box which can be destroyed
later, with warm blankets which will have
to be changed and washed from time to
time. Keep the cat in a warm room, with
ample ventilation. If the cat is able to get
out of the bed, a sanitary tray will have to
be provided. If the cat will not use this,
because it is trained to go out into the
garden, it may have to be carried out
there, carefully watched, and taken back
into the warm as quickly as possible. Sick
cats are inclined to crawl away under
some bush to die, so never leave one
unattended if it is really ill.

A good way to stop a cat scratching when
giving it medicine, is to wrap it in a
towel.

The cat will probably have to be given
medicines as prescribed by the vet. If the
medicine is sticky, the face should be
gently wiped with dampened cotton wool
and dried with a soft towel. The cat may
be dirty under the tail, especially if
suffering with diarrhoea. It makes
cleaning easier if the fur under the tail
and down the legs is clipped short. It
should be washed, dried, and talcum-
powdered.

If the cat will eat at all, it should be
given a little of its favourite food, or
something with a strong flavour, provided
the vet agrees. Sardines or pilchards may
be a good idea. If it refuses all food, the
vet may be able to give it a suitable
injection. If the patient will drink water,
add a little glucose to help give it some
energy.

Talk to the cat constantly, and do not
leave it alone for hours; even a radio left
on in the room will make it feel that it is
not alone. Once it is obviously recovering,
feeding little and often may help it to regain
strength. As it recovers, if the weather
is fine, a walk around the garden may
cheer it up. If the cat is suffering from a
contagious illness, you must always wash
your hands after touching it; put on an
overall when attending to the cat; change
your shoes afterwards; and immediately
burn any cotton wool used. Never handle
any other cats or write to friends that
have cats and kittens.

You may have to give your cat a tablet
or a pill, and this is sometimes quite
difficult. The thing is to be quick about it.
If possible have someone on hand to
help. Take the cat in your arms and open
the mouth with the thumb and finger of
one hand, pressing gently. With the other
hand drop the pill right to the back of the
throat, pushing it down as far as possible
with a finger. Rub the cat's throat gently
until you are sure the pill has gone.

Left and below: Cats and kittens that have complete freedom will often pick up fleas and mites, especially from fields. The best way to get rid of them is to use a spray recommended by the vet as shown in the lower picture. You should check your kitten regularly to make sure that it has not caught fleas.

A to Z of ailments

There are a number of ailments that may affect cats, including:

ABSCESSES A scratch or a bite received in a fight with another cat is the most common cause of this. A tiny hole is made by a claw or a tooth, which closes up leaving dirt or bacteria inside. A hard swelling may be the first sign. The cat looks miserable, has a temperature and is off its food. If noticed in time, the vet may be able to give antibiotics that will get rid of the abscess. It may be necessary to bring it to a head with hot water fomentations, until it bursts. The water must not be so hot that it burns the animal. Once all the matter is out, try to keep the wound open as long as possible by daily bathing with warm water with a mild antiseptic in it, applying a dressing to keep it clean. The abscess may have to be lanced by the vet if it cannot be brought to a head fairly quickly. An abscess on the ear flap

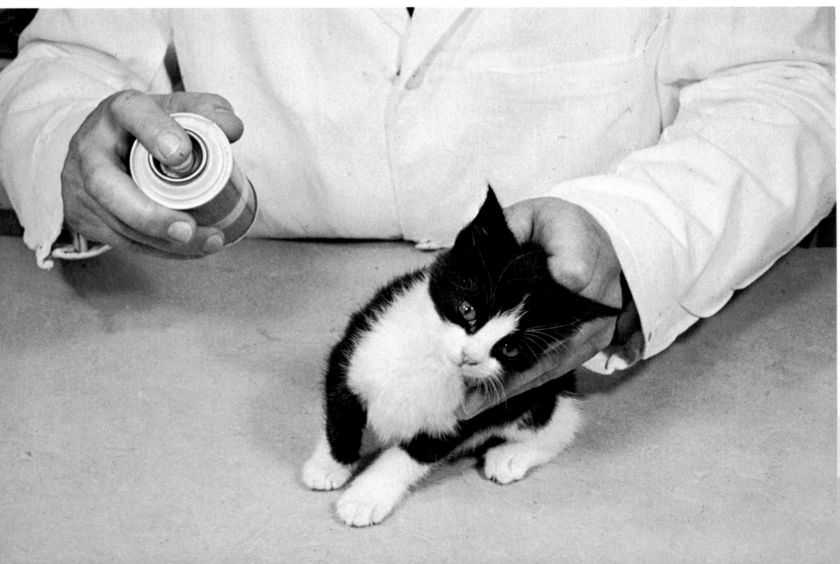

Parasites

As well as fleas there are other parasites such as lice, ticks and mites, that cats may pick up, especially those living in the country. Tiny and slow in movements, lice look like scurf, with the eggs or nits sticking glue-like to the fur. The vet will give a suitable preparation for treatment.

Ticks are bloodsuckers and are very debilitating. They are blue-grey in colour, cling to the skin, and swell up as they suck the blood. A drop of surgical spirit will make the jaws open, and you can pick them off with tweezers. The heads must not break off. Harvest mites look like tiny orange-red specks on the edges of the ears and between the toes. Most flea powders will destroy these.

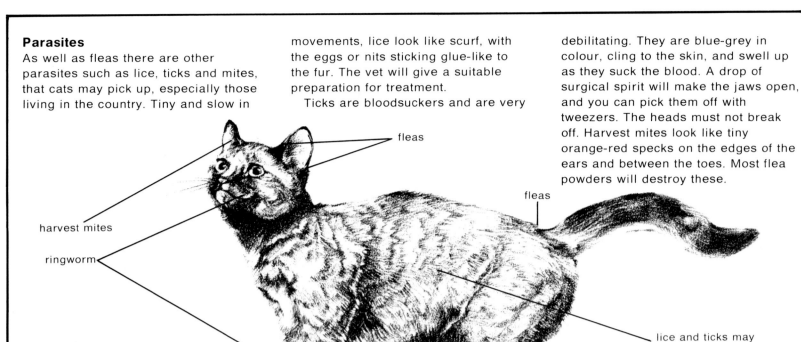

fleas
harvest mites
ringworm
harvest mites
fleas
lice and ticks may
be found
all over body

should have veterinary attention.

BLADDER TROUBLES If your cat seems to be having trouble in passing water, call in the vet at once as it may be cystitis, or inflammation of the bladder.

CONJUNCTIVITIS If the eyelid looks sore and inflamed and there is a discharge, bathe it gently to remove any matter. If it is not better the next day, see your vet who will prescribe suitable treatment. Conjunctivitis can be contagious so handle the cat with care, washing your hands well afterwards.

CONSTIPATION A kitten going to a new home, with a change of drinking water and food, may become constipated. A teaspoonful of liquid paraffin or olive oil may help this. Food should be moistened a little. Underfeeding may also cause constipation.

DIARRHOEA Cow's milk often causes this in a kitten or cat. In fact, some cats cannot take milk at all. Others can take tinned milk with a little water mixed. If the diarrhoea is persistent, it must be treated professionally.

EAR MITES These are often referred to as canker, and may take several forms. If a cat starts shaking its head and scratching around the ears, look inside to see if there is any brownish matter or if there is

The kitten's ears should be regularly examined to prevent earmites. Proprietary brands of 'canker powder' should *never* be put into the ear, as they dry out the healthy moisture.

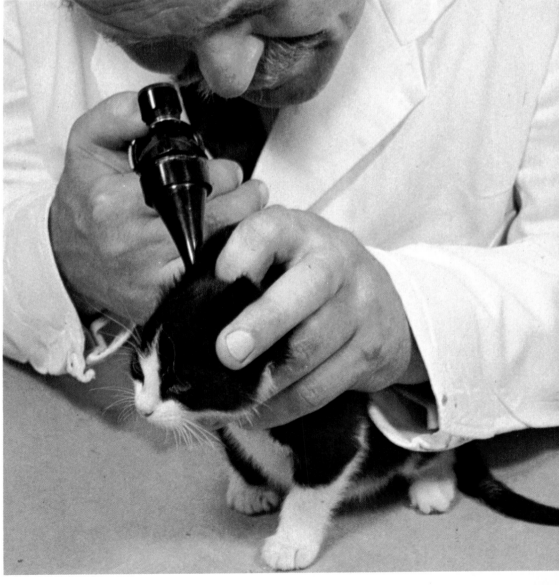

Emergency first aid

If you suspect that a cat has had an accident or received an injury, it should be kept still and moved as little as possible. A towel or small blanket may be used as a stretcher and, with help, the animal can be gently laid on it, placed in the back of a car and taken to a vet. If you have one, you could use a box that is small enough to restrict movement. Even if the cat appears to be unconscious, it may still be able to hear its owner's voice. The owner should keep talking in a reassuring way.

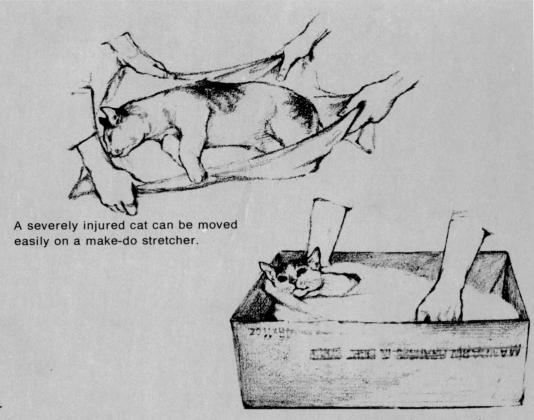

A severely injured cat can be moved easily on a make-do stretcher.

Bandaging an injured limb to keep it immobile.

If shock is suspected, wrap cat in a thick blanket and keep it warm.

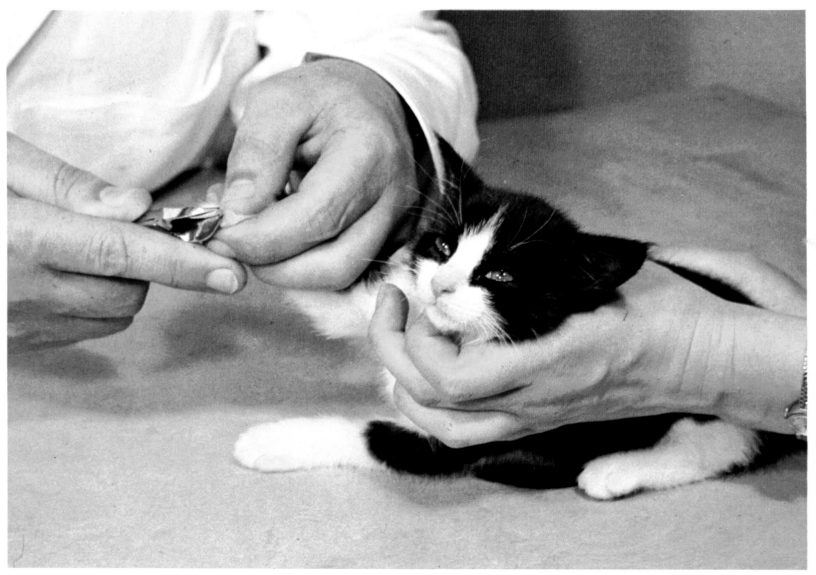

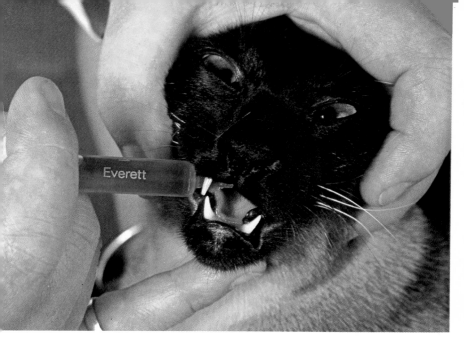

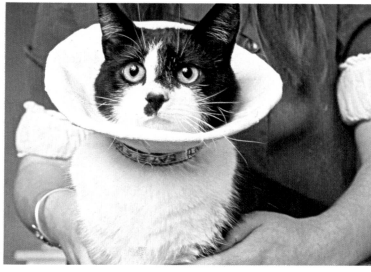

Above and right: Liquid medicine can be squirted into the mouth with a pen filler or a syringe. To give tablets, press on both sides of the mouth to keep it open, and push the tablet to the back of the throat. *Above far right:* This cat is wearing an Elizabethan collar to prevent it scratching a wound.

a smell. Clean out the ears very thoroughly (being careful not to poke deeply) with cotton wool soaked in olive oil, then apply ear drops. There are several on the market, but if the trouble still persists it may be cheaper in the long run to get the correct treatment from your vet.

ECZEMA This is not a contagious disease. It may be caused by an allergy, such as being allergic to fish or milk. There are various forms, some causing irritation, which makes the cat keep scratching so that sores form. A vet must examine the cat to diagnose the particular type of eczema before it can be properly treated. If it is caused by some food it may be possible to trace it eventually.

FLEAS A cat should not be allowed to have fleas, and daily grooming is a must to get rid of them. Fleas can cause a cat to scratch constantly and may start skin troubles and worms. Little grit-like black specks in the fur are the flea excreta. Flea powder or spray recommended for cats should be used once a week until the cat is completely free. (Never use on young kittens.) Sprinkle powder in the fur and brush it out completely. The sleeping box and the bedding should be disinfected.

FRACTURES A cat does not always land on

Left: This kitten is having the little sharp tips of its claws clipped. It is rarely necessary to cut a cat's claws if it can strop on trees or a scratching post. If they do have to be clipped, it should be done the proper way by a vet. Cutting too deep can cause severe bleeding and is very painful for the cat.

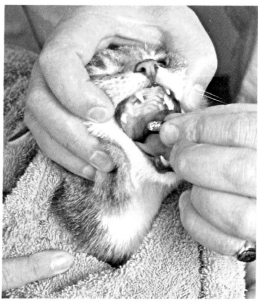

his feet after a fall. It can be killed or break a limb. An accident, such as being hit by a car, can fracture a leg. The tail may be broken by shutting in a door. Never attempt to put a splint on it yourself. Move the cat as little as possible and get professional treatment immediately.

FURBALL or HAIRBALL If the cat is not groomed frequently, it may lick and swallow the old hairs in the fur. A weekly dose of liquid paraffin or corn oil put in a saucer for it to lick may make the hair pass through the cat, or eating grass may make him vomit it up. If the stomach feels hard and swollen, you should suspect furball, which may need treatment. Never give castor oil as this is not at all suitable for cats.

LIMPING If your cat limps around or holds one paw in the air, look at the pads in case it has picked up a thorn. This can be removed with tweezers and the paw bathed. If the pad has been badly cut by broken glass or a sharp object, bathe the wound. If it is deep it may require a stitch or two.

POISONS A cat can become seriously or fatally ill through licking or swallowing

something poisonous. Lead paint, disinfectants containing creosote, weed-killers, strychnine or a similar poison can all kill cats. If the mouth is not burned, a piece of washing soda pushed down the throat, or salt and water, may make the cat sick, bringing up the poison. If the poison is an irritant, give a little milk. In any case, rush the animal to the vet if poisoning is suspected.

SKIN TROUBLES There are several skin ailments from which a cat may suffer. Ringworm is one of them. It is a horrible thing as it can be given to the cat by the owner or it can be caught from the cat. If you notice bald circular patches in the fur, get professional advice, and wear rubber gloves to handle the cat. It was once thought almost impossible to treat ringworm in cats, but it is now easier to deal with, although it may take time. It is important that the cat is isolated and young children, who are particularly susceptible, should not be allowed to come into contact with it until it is cured.

STINGS A cat may paw at a bee or wasp and be stung. A bee sting should be removed with a pair of tweezers. Apply a paste of bicarbonate of soda and water to reduce the swelling. A sting in the mouth should be treated by the vet.

WORMS There are two kinds of worms which may affect cats and kittens. These are roundworms and tapeworms. The roundworms which may be found in kittens look like pieces of string and can cause mild or severe illness. If the fur clings to the sides, with the kitten looking off-colour, possibly with the haws, or third eyelid, up in the corners of the eyes, the kitten probably needs worming. Adult cats can have roundworms, but this is not as serious as it is in kittens.

Tapeworms in a cat (rare in a young kitten) may be seen under the tail. They look like grains of rice. The cat may have a ravenous appetite, but still looks in very poor condition. It is sensible to consult the vet, not to buy preparations yourself.

Chapter eight
Breeding and Rearing Kittens

Rearing kittens is a demanding job and the costs involved are high. Don't forget that if your cat is not a pedigree breed, you may have difficulty in finding homes for the kittens.

Breeding kittens is not a hobby to be entered into lightly. It is not simply a question of buying male and female pedigree kittens and waiting for them to grow up to produce kittens exactly like themselves.

Male and female cats mature at different ages. The female may be ready to have kittens before the male is fully developed; or the other way round, with the female not fully grown but the male quite an adult.

Keeping a male unfortunately means that eventually he will have to have his own cat house and big run in the garden. He may be able to be kept indoors until he is one or even two years old, but after that he will probably spray urine about, leaving a horrible tomcat smell around the house. It is unfair to treat a kitten as a pet and then to put him outside all alone when he is grown up.

If you want to start breeding it is a better idea to buy a very good female and to send her away to a stud to be mated when she is old enough and big enough. A female 'calls' when she is in season and is ready to be mated. She will probably be ready to go to a stud when she is about a year old and when she has called at least twice. It is not possible to know exactly when a female will come into season for the first time, or how often this will happen afterwards.

Different varieties mature at different ages. The Foreign cats, such as Siamese, are usually old enough to have kittens before Longhairs. Some Siamese may think they are old enough when only five months old and Longhairs when about seven months old, but this is far too young.

The mating with a suitable male will have to be booked well in advance. The first sign is often when the female becomes even more friendly than usual, and there is a slight swelling of the sexual organs under the tail. She may go off her food and start almost crooning, and then letting out an occasional yell. Some really howl at the top of their voices, frightening their owners, and sometimes the neighbours too. She must be kept in to make sure that she does not meet any strange males before she goes away to be mated.

A female can have a litter of kittens and then be spayed or neutered later on if you do not wish her to have any more.

Young kittens soon become sturdy enough to climb out of their box and set off to explore the big world beyond. They are very inquisitive and take an interest in everything they see.

The stud owner will make all the arrangements about mating the female. If by any chance she does not have kittens as a result it is possible for her to go back to the same male. A stud fee will be payable in advance.

When the female returns home, you must not treat her like an invalid. From the time of the mating it will be at least 65 days, or even 67, before the kittens arrive. The mother-to-be must be allowed to live a perfectly normal life, with a good mixed diet, but not over-fed as she may become too fat and have trouble in

Left: This is the usual way for a mother cat to carry a tiny kitten. It is all right for very small kittens to be carried like this, but you should never pick up an older kitten or a cat this way as the muscles at the back of the neck can easily be torn. *Right:* A comfortable bed should be provided for the mother cat and her young family, preferably in the shade and out of any draughts.

Left: Newborn kittens may need the extra warmth of a hot water bottle wrapped in a blanket if the mother is taking a long time to have the litter. Cover the kittens with part of the blanket too. Mother and kittens should be kept warm and out of draughts. *Below left:* Kittens are blind at birth, and their ears are flat to their heads. They cannot do very much for the first week or so.

having her kittens. For the last week or two, she should not be allowed to climb trees or to jump to very high surfaces, as the extra weight may make her misjudge the distances.

The birth of the kittens

When the time of kittening draws near, the cat may start going around looking for what she considers is a suitable place in which to have her babies. This could be in a cupboard, or a drawer, or even in your bed. It is best to have a cardboard box ready, with plenty of newspaper in it. It should be big enough for her to stretch out in, but not so big that the kittens get far away from her and become cold. It should be placed in a secluded corner in a dim light, away from draughts, where the mother will not be disturbed unduly.

Show the mother cat the box several times. She will probably get into it and may tear the paper into shreds, making a cosy bed. After the kittens have all been born, if she does not mind them being handled, the torn-up paper can be removed. Replace it with a thick blanket that will not ruck up easily and cover the kittens so that the mother cannot find them.

Most cats have their kittens with no trouble at all. In fact your cat may have hers in the night without you knowing, but it is better, particularly for a first litter, for someone to be around to keep an eye on her. If one kitten arrives and the mother is busy attending to the next, it is as well to put a covered hot-water bottle in the box to keep the small creature warm.

It is important for the first few days at least that the kittens should be in a warm room, with the temperature about 70 F (21 C). Kittens are born blind, but still manage by instinct to crawl to the mother and to start suckling her milk. If she seems to be straining unduly for an hour or so, and no kittens arrive, it is as well to telephone the vet.

If the mother cat has no milk it may be necessary to hand feed the kittens, but this is a very demanding job as they will need feeding every two hours day and night for the first week or two. Cow's milk is not really suitable for kittens, but goat's milk can be given if it is possible to get it.

Taking a cat to stud

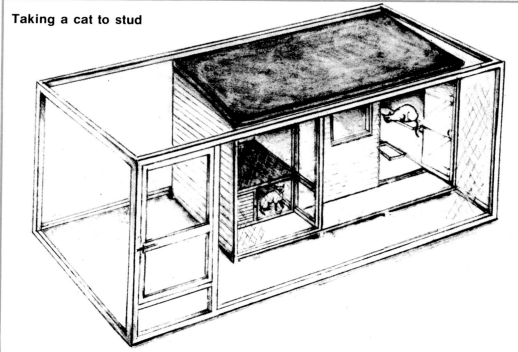

not mind them being handled. The best way is to hold the kitten comfortably in your hand with the tail towards you. Under the tail a male will have a little circular opening with a small slit and a crumbled effect about half an inch away, while the female has a small circular opening with a small slit close to it. It is easier to compare and identify the two sexes, if there are both males and female in the litter.

For the first three weeks, the mother should be able to look after the kittens entirely, but you must watch to make sure that all seem to be feeding well, and that one is not being more greedy than the others. The eyes start to open when the kittens are about ten to twelve days old, but this does vary considerably according to the variety. If the lids look swollen and fail to open, wipe them very, very gently with a little dampened cotton wool, and put a little Vaseline on them. The vet should certainly be asked to see the kittens if their eyes still fail to open after a day or two.

At the age of about three weeks the kittens will be climbing out of the box, and a low litter tray can then be provided. They will soon start to use it once they have been put on it a few times and this is the start of training them to be clean in the house. Weaning may also start at about this time by giving a proprietary brand of food for kittens of this age, or evaporated milk mixed with warm water. Put a drop on the tip of your finger at first and see if the kittens are interested. They may try to lick it off. Next time put about half a teaspoonful to their mouths, but never force it. After

Before booking up for your female to go to a stud to be mated, you should certainly go along to see the male. Ask to see his quarters, which should be quite clean, with no smell or dirty litter trays about. Ideally, all surfaces should be washable.

There should be a separate wired-off section for the female in the stud house. This will probably be a compartment about 6 ft (2 m) long by 3 ft (1 m) wide and 3 ft (1 m) high. One end should be a separate sleeping compartment with a solid door, so that the female has some privacy; the other end should form a wire run for her to see through and talk to the male. The top should be solid so that the male can jump on the roof and look through the wire. You should take a familiar blanket for the female to sleep on, as this will remind her of home.

Unlike dogs, which may be mated immediately when taken to stud, a cat will probably have to stay for several days. Most stud owners like to take the female in on the second day of her call, or coming into season. On no account let her out for a week at least on her return from the stud.

It is possible to buy a proprietary brand of substitute milk made especially for kittens and cats. Mix it to the correct strength and give it to the kitten a drop at a time with a syringe or with a small baby bottle, or one bought specially for this purpose.

When all the kittens have arrived safely, give the mother a warm drink and leave her with her new family. If the kittens are mongrels and you cannot find homes for them and so have to destroy them, do not destroy them all. Let her keep at least one, otherwise she might be very miserable and may also suffer pain with no kittens to suck the milk.

Looking after young kittens

Sexing may be done when the kittens are two or three days old if the mother does

After about ten days the eyes open and the ears begin to prick up. The eyes are dark blue until the kitten is about six weeks old, when they start to turn to their final colour.

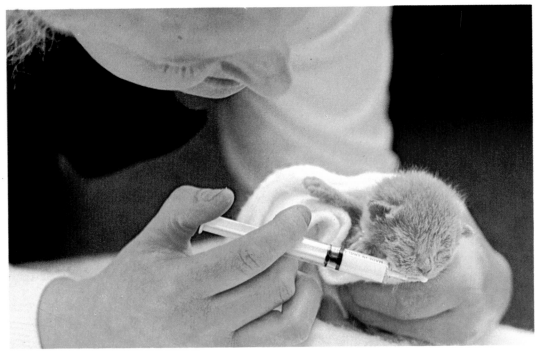

about a week they should start lapping from a small saucer, with one or two teaspoonsful of the mixture in it. Feed the kittens separately to make sure that all get their fair share. A few drops of milk of magnesia in the food will help them to digest the milk. After a week or so the milk food should be increased, and a little cooked minced rabbit, scraped raw beef or mashed up white fish may be given. The strained foods given to babies are very good.

If the mother cat has died, or has no milk, it is possible to bring up a kitten by hand-feeding it. *Left:* A newborn kitten can be fed with a syringe. It is quite a task as the kitten has to be fed every two hours for the first week or two. *Below:* As the kitten grows, you can use a doll's feeding bottle, or one made especially for kittens.

Finding new homes

At about seven to eight weeks, the kittens should be fully weaned, and be having four or five meals a day. They should be self-reliant, and able to run about all over the place. It is usual nowadays not to sell pedigree kittens until they are about twelve weeks old. By this time they are able to have their injections against Feline Infectious Enteritis and should be on a mixed diet. They should also be house-trained. Mongrel kittens mature earlier and most can leave home when they are about eight or nine weeks old. The mother will be a little upset when the kittens are old enough to go, and it is better for her if you let them leave one at a time, not all at once. Some mothers get fed up with their kittens and do get a little spiteful with them, especially when they still try to feed from her and she feels their sharp needle-like teeth.

If the kittens are pedigree and are not already booked, it is as well to start advertising them a week or two before they are old enough to go. Specialist cat magazines, which you can order from a newsagent, carry advertisements for pedigree cats and kittens. You can also try local newspapers. Always try to find out as much as you can about the would-be owner to make sure that the kitten will be going to a good home where it will be well looked after.

Mongrel kittens can be advertised on notice boards outside shops or in pet shops, or in local newspapers. Friends may be willing to take a kitten. Never advertise kittens for free. Ask for a small sum which you can give to the animal welfare societies if you like. Never sell or give a kitten to a small child that comes to the door, saying that his mother says he may have one. Ask the child to come

Above: The mother cat will carry her kittens to different places and sometimes makes a new nest for them in a place of her own choosing. *Right:* This four to five week old kitten looks very determined. It is clearly out on a journey of discovery!

back with his mother.

Whoever has the kittens, always give a diet sheet so that the new owners can give them more or less the same food. If the kittens are pedigree, they should be registered and the necessary documents should be provided with them when they are sold.

It is quite possible for the mother cat to start calling again, even while she is still feeding the kittens, or shortly after they have gone. She should certainly not be mated again immediately, but must be allowed to build up her strength and get into good condition. Most breeders allow their female cats only one, or possibly two, litters a year to ensure that the kittens they sell are strong and healthy.

Becoming a breeder

If you like the idea of breeding as a hobby, do remember that it does cost a great deal of money. Prices for prize-winning pedigree kittens may be rising all the time, but so too are the costs involved. Stud fees are high and may not always result in kittens being born. If there are kittens, they are not always good enough for showing. The vet's fees will be high, so is the cost of the various inoculations. Feeding becomes more expensive every day, and strong healthy stock must be well fed.

A stud cat is not happy if it is kept purely as a mate for one female. Unless you were planning to have three or four

females of your own, you would need to take in visiting females. Anyone who has to cope with visiting cats needs to be very responsible and also used to handling them. Female cats coming to stud, especially for the first time, are most unpredictable in their behaviour. Cats that may be very sweet at home can become very difficult in strange surroundings. Sometimes owners are absolutely shocked when they are told how their cats behaved. Some cats turn savage because they are very frightened. They may attack both the male and the stud owner, especially if the owner is trying to hold them. On the other hand, some cats are on their best behaviour all the time.

It is essential to provide the stud with a house that is absolutely escape-proof before accepting visitors, and to have some form of heating, as some females may never be allowed outside their own homes.

Chapter nine
Cat Shows

There are shows for every breed as well as for the everyday pet. To be the champion of its breed, a cat needs star treatment for weeks beforehand. As well as being the right shape and colour, it must be the picture of health on the day, with gleaming, well groomed fur.

The majority of cat shows are for pedigree cats, but a number do have a section especially for mongrels. The procedure for entering both sorts is very similar.

To show a pedigree cat it must be registered with the Governing Council of the Cat Fancy in Britain, or one of the nine governing bodies of cat registries in the United States. The Cat Fanciers' Association is the largest. A mongrel is not registered, and is of unknown or non-pedigree parentage.

Pedigree cats are judged by what the judge considers to be the nearest to the required standard for that particular variety (see Chapter 2). The perfect cat has yet to be born, so never be afraid to show your cat. It may be better than you think. There are many prizes and you may be agreeably surprised by the results. Pets are judged on their condition and the way they can be handled. If your pet is very nervous, frightened of strangers, and not very friendly, it is better not to enter it.

Cat shows are held all over the country, but it is sometimes difficult to find out when and where. Specialist cat magazines sometimes give lists and advertisements for shows, or you can find out about shows from the Governing Council of the Cat Fancy, or the Cat Fanciers' Association in the United States.

Entering for a show
Write to the show manager about two months before the date of the show, asking for a schedule and entry form, and saying whether your cat is a pedigree or just a pet. The entry form for a pet cat is very easy to fill in. It asks for a few particulars, such as the cat's name, approximate age, the colour and coat

A beautiful Red-point Siamese ready to go to the show, where he will undoubtedly be a winner, despite strong competition. The Siamese classes at the show are usually very well filled.

pattern. The schedule will give details of the classes, which are usually split up according to the colours. There may be other classes, such as the most unusual-looking; the biggest eyes; the best cat or kitten owned by a child; the cat with the sleekest coat or the most luxurious, and so on. Males over nine months must have been neutered, but this rule does not apply to females.

A pedigree cat must be registered, and if you are not a breeder, it must have been transferred to your ownership at least three weeks before the date of the show.

When the schedule arrives, read all the rules and regulations through very carefully, as any mistakes made on the entry form may result in your cat being disqualified.

You will see there are classes for every pedigree variety. Cats and kittens may be entered in from four to twelve classes. For your first show it is really better to enter your cat in only about four classes, so that you can see how it behaves and what the judges think of it.

The general details are much the same. Kittens must be three months of age at least and it is always recommended that all exhibits be vaccinated against Feline Infectious Enteritis. It is not cheap to enter a show. Exhibitors have to pay a benching fee for the cat's pen, which has to be hired by the cat club, and there is a fee for each class entered, plus the fee for a pass for you to enter the hall.

It is not necessary to belong to the club running the show, but if you are a member there is a slight reduction in the fees payable and special club classes. There are also classes put on by other clubs especially for their members.

If showing a pet cat, preparation must be started several weeks beforehand. It must be groomed regularly, so that on the day of the show, it looks a picture of health, with shining fur, no trace of fleas and no tangles or matts in the coat. The ears must be quite clean, with no sign of

This attractive kitten has done well at the show, and has been chosen as the best kitten. He is being held up so he can be clearly seen and receive the applause of his audience.

canker, and the eyes must be bright and sparkling, with no dirt in the corners. It is no use getting the cat out of the garden on the morning of the show and hoping that he will be a prizewinner. He may look perfect in your eyes, but remember that the judging will be strict, so he must look at his best if he is to be a winner.

Pedigree cats and kittens also need star treatment for weeks before a show if the judge is to be impressed.

The day of the show
Every cat or kitten entered for a show, whether pedigree or pet, is thoroughly examined by the veterinary surgeons, and if for any reason it is considered that your cat is not really in tip-top condition, or is running a temperature, or has dirty ears or fleas, you may not be allowed to exhibit him. He will then have to be penned in the special sick bay all day or – a much better plan – taken home straight away. All fees are then forfeited. It may seem hard, but it is for your cat's sake as well as all the other cats; even if they are vaccinated against Feline Infectious Enteritis, there are other illnesses which can be passed on from one cat to another, and a cat that is below par may well pick up an infection.

A week or two before the show, you will be sent a numbered disc, known as the tally. This has to be put on a piece of white tape and worn by the cat around its neck. There will also be a vetting-in card with the same number on it, which has to be handed to the veterinary surgeon before the examination.

Once past the vet you can heave a sigh of relief and take your exhibit into the hall. You will be confronted by rows and rows of pens, and will have to find the one which bears the same number as

Preparing for a show
It is not necessary to bath a shorthaired cat before a show, unless it is white. If it has to be done, bath it several days beforehand, so there is time for the natural grease to return to the fur.

Never groom until the fur is quite dry after a bath, then only use a soft brush and a narrow-toothed comb that will not leave tracks in the fur. Do make sure there are no fleas and the ears are clean.

Polish by hard hand stroking or rubbing with a piece of velvet, a chamois leather or a silk handkerchief until the fur is shining and glossy. Make sure the corners of the eyes are quite clean.

Get everything that the cat will need ready the night before the show. Include a hot water bottle if the weather's very cold. Do not let the cat out in the morning in case it vanishes.

A general view of a cat show. The exhibits wait in individual pens to be judged. Here, judging is still in progress – it usually goes on for most of the day. Results appear on an award board.

your cat's tally. It is as well to take with you some cotton wool slightly dampened with a mild disinfectant that is harmless to cats, and to wipe over the bars of the pen.

The show regulations will advise you to bring a plain white blanket, a sanitary tray with suitable litter, and feeding bowls for food and drink. These should also be white. If it is very cold, you may put a hot water bottle under the blanket, but it must be completely hidden. You also have to supply food and milk or water, but must not put the bowls in the pen until after lunch.

At cat shows in Britain, judging usually starts at about 10 o'clock, and may go on

until the late afternoon, depending on the number of cats entered. At most shows you have to leave the hall, but may watch from the gallery, but sometimes the public are allowed in all day. It is important not to go near the judge while he or she is judging your cat.

Showing in Great Britain
There are three kinds of shows which are organized by cat clubs under licence from

Above: A panel of senior judges examines the kittens nominated by the judges of the shorthair classes. These judges choose the best kitten in the show. *Right:* At this show in Europe, stewards bring the cats – the longhairs this time – to the judge for her assessment. This must be a moment of extreme tension for the owners of the cats, who await the results anxiously.

the Governing Council. The first and most important are Championship shows where challenge certificates are given to the first prize winners in the Open or Breed class for each adult variety.

A cat has to win three challenge certificates given by three different judges at three shows before it can be called a champion. Neuters may also compete in special classes, and three premier certificates awarded by three judges at three shows bestows on a cat the title of premier. There are also classes for champions only and classes for premiers only, and cats winning these classes at three shows under three different judges are entitled to be called Grand Champions and Grand Premiers.

The second kind of shows are the Sanction shows, which are run on exactly the same lines as those of the Championship shows, but no challenge

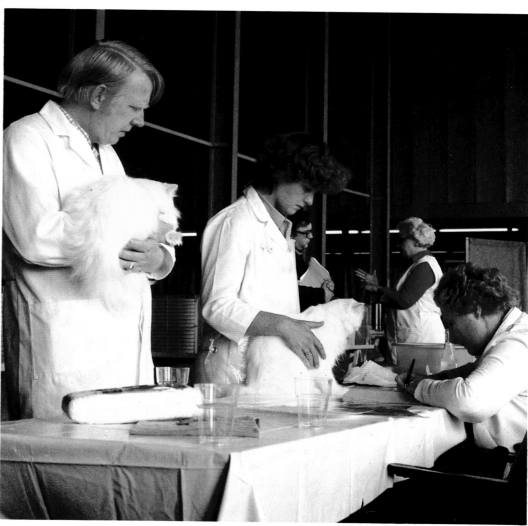

Above: The end of the day at the cat show. A winning exhibit proudly displays his winnings. *Right:* A beautiful example of a Tortie Colourpoint. It comes very close to the breed standard.

or premier certificates are given.

The third kind are the Exemption shows, which are usually small local shows, with fewer classes. Again, there are no challenge or premier certificates given, and there are fewer rules and regulations. These are excellent shows for beginners, as it gives them an insight into cat shows and their organization.

Some shows have panels of judges to choose the Best Cat, the Best Kitten and the Best Neuter in the show from the cats nominated by the various judges. Others choose the Best of Breed. Best of Breed means that the best cat and kitten of each variety – the ones which come closest to the required breed standard – are chosen and are given special cards and awards.

Showing in the United States
Shows in the United States differ in many ways from those held in Britain. The procedure beforehand is much the same, however. The would-be exhibitor applies for a form on which to enter the cat's name and registration details, and sends it in to the show manager with the correct money. But instead of paying for individual classes, the exhibitor pays one big entry fee. Some shows in Britain are now trying this method out, but the overall fee is quite high because there are so many classes – far more than in the United States.

There is the novice class (for cats that have never won a ribbon); the Open (for cats that have won before but are not champions); the Champion class (for champions only); and the Grand Champion class. The kitten class is for kittens between the ages of four and eight months.

The veterinary inspection at the show is the same as in Britain. The cat is taken into the show hall afterwards and placed in its pen. The judges do not go to the pens, so they can be decorated with curtains and any previously won ribbons. The setting is always very colourful.

Each judge stands or sits at a table, in front of a row of pens. The cats in each class are put in these pens for judging. The winner of the class is left to compete against those entered in the next class, and so on. A really outstanding exhibit can start as a novice and finish up as Best in Show.

Rows of chairs for the audience are placed in front of the judges and quite frequently a judge will tell them what she thinks of a particular cat and why she is giving the ribbon.

Ribbons are given to the Best of Colour, the Best Opposite Sex of Colour, the First in a class, the Best Champion and so on. The ribbon colour for a first prize winner is blue. For a second place it is red. In Britain it is the other way round. Prize money is not awarded, but cash and other awards are frequently offered by cat food manufacturers and other similar companies to the best exhibits.

The shows usually last two days. The Best is chosen on the second day, and the awards are given at the end of the show.

Quite frequently, three or four clubs combine to give a show, but each is run as a separate show with a judge for each. The cats are judged separately in each show, so a good cat can win a great number of ribbons.

There are about nine registered bodies in the States, all similar to the Governing Council in Britain. They all approve shows and, provided a cat is registered individually with the various bodies, the opportunity for exhibiting is much greater than in Britain. There are shows every week-end in different parts of the country, and owners travel miles to them.

Many friendships are made at cat shows, when exhibitors talk to one another about their cats, frequently going to one another's homes afterwards to see each other's kittens. If you are worried about showing your cat, it may be as well to visit a show first of all to find out what it is all about. If you intend to become a serious breeder, it is important that you show your kittens. If they do well and win prizes, you will become known in the Cat Fancy or Cat Fanciers' Association, and people will want to buy them. If you just want to show your mongrel pet, that should be looked on as fun and never taken too seriously. If your cat wins a rosette that will be wonderful. If he does not, you know that he is the best pet in the world anyway.

Index

Page numbers in italics
refer to illustrations.

Acknowledgements

The publishers would like to thank the following individuals and organisations for their kind permission to reproduce the pictures in this book:
Animal Graphics 1, 22, 38, 46, 73, 75; Animal Photography (Victor Baldwin) 4–5 (Peter Smith) 12, 46, 47 (Sally-Anne Thompson) 17, 19, 20, 27, 28, 29, 32, 36, 40, 45, 48, 50, 51, 53, 55, 57, 58, 60, 69, 71; Barnaby's 10; Bavaria-Verlag 44 (Kalt Gerolf) 24 (W Luthy) 55 (E Seake) 62; S C Bisserot 66; Camera Press 29, 47, 53, 67, 68; Bruce Coleman 18; Gerald Cubitt 2–3; Anne Cumbers 14–15, 15, 17, 31, 56, 57, 68, 70, 72, 77; F.P.G. 21; Jane Miller 52; John Moss endpapers, 13, 16, 22, 27, 30, 35, 37, 39, 41, 49, 59, 62, 63, 64; Musee de Louvre, Paris 7; Natural Science Photos 9, 10–11, Octopus Library 61, 65; Photo Research International 50; Angela Sayer 25, 74, 75, 76; Scala 8; Spectrum 13, 23, 34, 35, 40, 42, 43, 49, 52, 67, 70; Zefa 33, 71 (Lummer) 54; Zoological Society of London 6.